Cases in Healthcare Finance

SECOND EDITION

Cases in Healthcare Finance

SECOND EDITION

Includes Diskette with Student Case Models

LOUIS C. GAPENSKI

AUPHA
HAP

Your board, staff, or clients may also benefit from this book's insight. For more information on quantity discounts, contact the Health Administration Press Marketing Manager at (312) 424-9470.

07   06   05   04   03   5   4   3   2   1

Library of Congress Cataloging-in-Publication Data here

Gapenski, Louis C.
  Cases in healthcare finance / Louis C. Gapenski. — 2nd ed.
    p. cm.
  ISBN 1-56793-200-2 (alk. paper)
    1. Health facilities — Finance — Case studies. 2. Medical care — Finance — Case studies. I. Title.

RA971.3 .G367 2002
362.1'068'1 — dc21   2002027624

The paper used in this publication meets the minimum requirements of American National Standard for Information SciencesPermanence of Paper for Printed Library Materials, ANSI Z39.48-1984. ∞ ™

Project manager/Editor: Jane C. Williams; Book/Cover designer: Matt Avery; Acquisitions editor: Marcy McKay

Health Administration Press
A division of the Foundation of the American
    College of Healthcare Executives
One North Franklin Street, Suite 1700
Chicago, IL 60606
(312) 424-2800

Association of University Programs
    in Health Administration
730 11th Street, NW
4th Floor
Washington, DC 20001
(202) 638-1448

Contents

Capital Investment

Working Capital

Other Topics

Ethics Mini-Cases

Preface

Healthcare finance can be a fascinating, exciting subject, yet students often regard it as either too theoretical or too mechanical. The fact is good financial decision making requires both good theory and good quantitative work plus a great deal of insight and judgment. The best way to get this point across to students, and to demonstrate the inherent richness of the subject matter, is to relate classroom work to real-world decision making. When this is done, students must not only grapple with the concepts but, more importantly, with how the concepts are applied in practice.

Of course, the most realistic application of occurs within healthcare organizations, and there is no substitute for "on-the-job" experience. The next best thing, and the only real option for the classroom, is to use cases to simulate, to the extent possible, the environment in which finance decisions are actually made. The purpose of this casebook is to provide students with an opportunity to bridge the gap between learning concepts in a lecture setting and actually applying them on the job. By using these cases, students can be better prepared to deal with the multitude of problems that arise in the practice of healthcare finance.

Content

This casebook primarily consists of 30 cases that focus on the practice of healthcare finance within provider organizations. In general, each case addresses a single financial issue, such as a capital investment decision, but the uncertainty of the input data, along with the presence of relevant nonfinancial factors, make each case interesting and challenging. Because the cases focus both on accounting and financial management decisions, they cover the full range of healthcare finance. Furthermore, the case settings include a wide variety of provider organizations, including hospitals, clinics, medical practices, and home health care organizations, as well as integrated delivery systems and managed care organizations.

In addition to healthcare finance cases, the casebook contains six ethics mini-cases. Each mini-case contains a very short description of a finance situation that has potential ethical implications. These cases require no numerical analysis; rather, they are intended to be used as discussion vehicles if instructors want to introduce finance-related ethics content in a finance course.

Changes from the First Edition

I have used the first edition in more than ten courses since its publication. Moreover, I have received comments and suggestions from numerous users in different settings. This feedback has resulted in many changes; a few are substantial and a great deal are minor. Perhaps the most substantial change is the addition of four cases.

- Case 9 (Christchurch Transplant Center) focuses on marginal cost pricing and outlier protection.
- Case 10 (Gotham Health Network) gives students the opportunity to conduct an activity based costing (ABC) analysis.
- Case 25 (Desert View Health System) involves the analysis of the use of physician extenders.
- Case 26 (Metropolitan University Hospital) focuses on the evaluation of two competing technologies, including backfill and replacement project analyses.

In addition, many other smaller changes have been made to improve both the cases and the models. Regarding the cases, the names were changed on all cases, and story and numerical changes were made to most cases to improve their teaching value. Regarding the models, many small changes were made to make the models easier to understand and to use. In addition, a model was created for Case 7

(Venture Mental Health: Variance Analysis) because several users indicated that the calculations required by the case were too tedious to perform by hand.

Directed Versus Nondirected Cases

In general, cases may be classified as *directed* or *nondirected*. Directed cases include a specific set of questions that students must answer to complete the case, while nondirected cases (as I use the term) contain only general guidance to point students in the right direction. Most of the cases in this casebook are nondirected. (Cases 11 through 14, which focus on basic finance concepts rather than applications, are directed.) The primary advantage of nondirected cases is that they closely resemble how real-world managers confront financial decision making because they require students to develop their own solution approach. The disadvantage is that students who stray from the key issues of the case often do not obtain full value from their effort.

In general, students with more advanced finance skills gain the most from nondirected cases, while students who have had less finance exposure gain most from directed cases. The Instructor's Manual for this casebook contains a set of case questions for each nondirected case that can be used to convert the nondirected cases into directed cases. Thus, instructors have the option of using the nondirected cases in either way, depending on the experience of the students, the objectives of the course, and the extent to which cases will be used.

Use of This Casebook

I have used the cases in this book in several alternative ways. First, these cases form the foundation for the required healthcare finance course in the University of Florida's MHA program. Students in this program take the MBA core accounting and finance sequence, so the healthcare finance course focuses on the application of finance concepts within health services organizations. The course is essentially a pure case course, and about 12 cases (one per week) are assigned. The students have had sufficient lecture work in finance, and at this stage learning by doing is most important. I do not provide students with the accompanying case questions, so they must develop their own approaches to completing each case.

A group of about three to four students is assigned to present each assigned case in class. Group work is an excellent experience for students because almost all decision making in businesses is done in a group environment, and people who cannot work in groups are doomed to failure. Students will need to know how to motivate people who work for them, and students will need to be able to work with others in a cooperative manner. Many students wish that they did not have to work in groups because doing their own thing at their own convenience is much easier. Because the world does not work that way, learning to work with others is better done now while mistakes are less costly. Typically, the highest-quality case analyses are conducted by cooperative teams that discuss the issues and methods. Generally, some team members will be good at computer modeling, others will be good writers or good with word processing or presentation software, while others will be good at identifying and analyzing the relevant points in the cases. By combining those talents, the group can produce a better case analysis than can one person working individually.

An in-class group presentation of the cases also provides students the opportunity to hone their presentation skills, including the use of presentation software such as Microsoft PowerPoint®. Healthcare executives constantly state that the ability to communicate is absolutely critical to success in business. I agree completely. A knowledge of healthcare finance (or any other managerial discipline) is useless unless the individual can communicate his or her ideas to others. Students who are not presenting the case must work the case individually, and then act as members of the board of directors (or trustees) during the presentation. They are responsible for asking relevant questions of the presenting group and pointing out any deficiencies in the analysis.

In addition to the healthcare finance course in our traditional program, I also teach a two-course sequence in the Executive MHA program. In essence, the first course covers healthcare accounting, while the second course covers capital finance. I use six to eight cases in each of these courses, which the students must work between the on-campus sessions and then make presentations in the same way as in the traditional program. I find that the Executive MHA students generally bring a great deal of real-world insights into their case analyses, which often makes the discussions livelier than those in the traditional program.

Spreadsheet Models

Spreadsheet analysis has become extremely important in all aspects of healthcare finance. Students must be given the opportunity to develop computer skills and be allowed, or required, to use spreadsheet programs to assist in case analyses. If students have not previously learned about spreadsheets, they must be exposed to them because "functional literacy" in any area of management today means at least some knowledge of spreadsheet modeling. Furthermore, spreadsheet models can reduce the amount of "busywork" required to perform the required calculations and hence leave students with more time to focus on finance issues.

Because of these factors, I developed well-structured, user-friendly spreadsheet models for those cases where models would help to create a more efficient analysis. Most of the cases could, of course, be done with only a calculator, but the spreadsheet models are far more efficient and hence big time savers, especially when conducting risk assessment using techniques such as sensitivity and scenario analyses. In addition, spreadsheet models allow students to easily create graphics and other computer output that enhance the quality of both the analyses and the presentations.

In thinking about student use of these models, an important question arose: Should I provide complete models to the students, or do I require students to do some (or all) of the modeling themselves? After using several different approaches, I concluded that that best solution is to provide students with complete versions of the case models in the sense that no modeling is required to obtain a *base case* solution. However, zeros have been entered for all input data in the student versions, and hence students must identify and then enter the appropriate input data. When this is done, the model automatically calculates the base case solution. However, the models do not contain risk analyses or other extensions such as graphics, so students must modify the models as necessary to make them most useful in completing the cases. The student versions of the case models are distributed with the casebook, so when students buy the casebook they also receive the student version case models.

The instructor versions of the case models are similar to the student versions, except that the input values are intact. Thus, instructors can view the base case solution without entering any data. In addition, some instructor version models have additional modeling such as risk analyses included. Both the Instructor's Manual and the instructor's case models are posted on Health Administration Press's instructors-only web page. Contact jking@ache.org to gain access to these files.

Spreadsheet models are available for 20 of the 30 cases. The ten cases without models are as follows:

Case 2   Peach State Health Plans: Assessing HMO Performance
Case 3   Maricopa Healthcare Eisenhower: Cost Allocation
          Concepts
Case 9   Christchurch Transplant Center: Marginal Cost Pricing
          Analysis
Case 11   Puget Sound Surgery Centers: Time Value Analysis
Case 12   University Medical Foundation, Inc.: Financial Risk
Case 13   Chesapeake Healthcare (A): Bond Valuation
Case 14   Chesapeake Healthcare (B): Stock Valuation
Case 15   Gold Coast Homecare: Cost of Capital
Case 25   Desert View Health System: Physician Extender Analysis
Case 30   Golden Gate Healthcare: Capitation and Risk Sharing

Some of these cases (2, 3, 9, 15, 25, and 30) do not require repetitive calculations, and hence there is no need for a model. The remaining cases (11, 12, 13, and 14) focus on basic principles that underlie mathematical calculations, and hence the best way to learn these principles is to perform the calculations by hand.

Acknowledgments

This casebook reflects the efforts of many people. Colleagues, students, and staff at the University of Florida provided inspirational support, as well as more tangible support, during the development and class testing of the revised cases. In addition, the Health Administration Press staff was instrumental in ensuring the quality and usefulness of this casebook.

Finally, four of the cases were coauthored by colleagues at the University of Florida or at Shands Healthcare, an affiliate of the University of Florida.

- Murray Côté coauthored Case 28, Platte River Hospital: Inventory Management.
- Ian Jamieson coauthored Case 9, Christchurch Transplant Center: Marginal Cost Pricing Analysis.
- Brett Justice coauthored Case 26, Metropolitan University Hospital: Competing Technologies with Backfill.
- Paul Phillips coauthored Case 25, Desert View Health System: Physician Extender Analysis.

I would not have been able to realize all of the improvements in this edition without their help.

Conclusion

The field of healthcare finance continues to undergo significant changes and advances. Participating in these developments is stimulating, and I sincerely hope that the second edition of *Cases in Healthcare Finance* will help you gain a better appreciation for the application of finance principles to health services organizations.

A book that raises so many issues will also inevitably generate a variety of opinions regarding both financial theory and practice. Furthermore, although both the publisher and I have placed great emphasis on the accuracy of the cases, some discrepancies or inconsistencies may likely exist. I would appreciate any comments, corrections, criticisms, and ideas for improving all aspects of the cases and related materials. Also, if any technical problems arise with the models, feel free to contact me directly.

Professor Louis C. Gapenski
Department of Health Services Administration
Box 100195, Health Science Center
University of Florida
Gainesville, FL 32610-0195
E-mail: gapenski@hp.ufl.edu

Financial Accounting

EASTSIDE MEMORIAL HOSPITAL (A)
ASSESSING HOSPITAL PERFORMANCE

EASTSIDE MEMORIAL HOSPITAL is a 210-bed, not-for-profit, acute care hospital with a long-standing reputation for providing quality healthcare services to a growing service area. Eastside competes with three other hospitals in its metropolitan statistical area (MSA)—two not-for-profit and one for-profit. Eastside is the smallest of the four but has traditionally been ranked highest in patient satisfaction polls.

Hospitals are accredited by JCAHO (Joint Commission on Accreditation of Healthcare Organizations), which is an independent not-for-profit organization sponsored by a number of professional and industry organizations such as the American Hospital Association (AHA) and the American Medical Association (AMA). (For more information on the Joint Commission, visit their web site at www.jcaho.org.) Although accreditation is optional for hospitals, it is generally required to qualify for governmental (Medicare and Medicaid) reimbursement, and hence the vast majority of hospitals apply for accreditation. Eastside passed its latest Joint Commission accreditation with "flying colors," receiving an Accreditation with Full Standards Compliance, the highest of eight accreditation categories.

In recent years, competition among the four hospitals in Eastside's service area has been keen, but friendly. However, a large for-profit chain recently purchased the for-profit hospital, which has resulted in some anxiety among the managers of the other three hospitals because of the chain's reputation for aggressively increasing market share in the markets they serve.

Relevant financial and operating data for Eastside are contained in Tables 1.1 through 1.4, and selected industry data are contained in Tables 1.5 and 1.6. (Note that the industry data given in the case are for illustrative purposes only and do not represent actual data for the years specified. For a better idea of the type of comparative data actually available for hospitals, see the Ingenix web site at www.hospitalbenchmarks.com.)

In addition, the following information was extracted from the notes section of Eastside's 2002 Annual Report.

1. A significant portion of the hospital's net patient service revenue was generated by patients who are covered either by Medicare, Medicaid, or other government programs or by various private plans, including managed care plans, which have contracts with the hospital that specify discounts from charges. In general, the proportional amount of deductions is similar between inpatients and outpatients. The gross/net revenue breakdown for both inpatient and outpatient services is given below (in millions of dollars):

	1998	1999	2000	2001	2002
Gross patient service revenue					
Inpatient	$25.161	$25.275	$26.117	$29.148	$33.216
Outpatient	4.748	5.969	6.535	9.130	11.912
Gross patient revenue	$29.909	$31.244	$32.652	$38.278	$45.128
Revenue deductions					
Contractual allowances	$ 2.489	$ 2.053	$ 1.729	$ 5.196	$ 7.516
Charity care	1.759	1.955	2.127	2.506	3.030
Total deductions	$ 4.248	$ 4.008	$ 3.856	$ 7.702	$10.546
Net patient service revenue	$25.661	$27.236	$28.796	$30.576	$34.582

2. Inventories are stated at the lower of cost, determined on a first-in, first-out basis, or market value.

3. The breakdown of operating expenses between inpatient and outpatient activities for 1998 through 2002 is as follows (in millions of dollars):

	1998	1999	2000	2001	2002
Inpatient expenses	$18.635	$19.221	$20.573	$22.229	$24.771
Outpatient expenses	5.261	6.062	6.831	8.098	9.187
Total operating expenses	$23.896	$25.283	$27.404	$30.327	$33.958

4. Eastside has a contributory money accumulation
    (defined contribution) pension plan, which covers
    substantially all of its employees. Participants can
    contribute up to 20 percent of earnings to the pension
    plan. The hospital matches on a dollar-for-dollar basis
    employee contributions of up to 2 percent of wages,
    and it pays 50 cents on the dollar for contributions

	1998	1999	2000	2001	2002
Revenues					
Net patient service revenue	$25.661	$27.236	$28.796	$30.576	$34.582
Other revenue	1.305	1.261	1.237	1.853	1.834
Total revenues	$26.966	$28.497	$30.033	$32.429	$36.416
Expenses					
Salaries and wages	$10.829	$11.135	$12.245	$12.468	$13.994
Fringe benefits	1.496	1.731	1.830	2.408	2.568
Interest expense	1.341	1.305	1.181	1.598	1.776
Depreciation	1.708	1.977	2.350	2.658	2.778
Provision for bad debts	0.546	0.589	0.622	0.655	0.776
Professional liability	0.102	0.157	0.140	0.201	0.218
Other	7.874	8.389	9.036	10.339	11.848
Total expenses	$23.896	$25.283	$27.404	$30.327	$33.958
Excess of revenues over expenses	$ 3.070	$ 3.214	$ 2.629	$ 2.102	$ 2.458

TABLE 1.1
Statements of
Operations
(millions of dollars)

TABLE 1.2
Balance Sheets
(millions of dollars)

	1998	1999	2000	2001	2002
Assets					
Cash and investments	$ 3.513	$ 5.799	$ 4.673	$ 5.069	$ 2.795
Accounts receivable (net)	5.915	4.832	4.359	5.674	7.413
Inventories	0.338	0.403	0.432	0.523	0.601
Other current assets	0.693	0.294	0.308	0.703	0.923
Total current assets	$10.459	$11.328	$ 9.772	$11.969	$11.732
Gross plant and equipment	$37.999	$42.005	$47.786	$55.333	$59.552
Accumulated depreciation	8.831	10.092	11.820	14.338	17.009
Net plant and equipment	$29.168	$31.913	$35.966	$40.995	$42.543
Total assets	$39.627	$43.241	$45.738	$52.964	$54.275
Liabilities and Net Assets					
Accounts payable	$ 1.068	$ 1.273	$ 0.928	$ 1.253	$ 1.760
Accruals	1.085	1.311	1.804	1.823	1.473
Current portion of LT debt	0.136	0.290	0.110	1.341	1.465
Total current liabilities	$ 2.289	$ 2.874	$ 2.842	$ 4.417	$ 4.698
Long-term debt	15.959	15.775	15.673	19.222	17.795
Net assets	21.379	24.592	27.223	29.325	31.782
Total liabilities and net assets	$39.627	$43.241	$45.738	$52.964	$54.275

over 2 percent and up to 4 percent. Because the plan is a defined contribution plan (as opposed to a defined benefit plan), there are no unfunded pension liabilities. Pension expense was approximately $0.543 million in 2001 and $0.588 million in 2002.

5. The hospital is a member of the State Hospital Trust Fund under which it purchases professional liability insurance coverage for individual claims up to $1 million (subject to a deductible of $100,000 per claim). Eastside is self-insured for amounts above $1 million, but less than $5 million. Any liability award in excess of $5 million is covered by a commercial liability policy; for example, the policy pays $2 million on a $7 million award. The hospital is currently involved in

	1999	2000	2001	2002	
					TABLE 1.3
					Statements of
Cash Flows from Operating Activities					**Cash Flows**
Income from operations	$3.214	$2.629	$2.102	$2.458	**(millions of dollars)**
Noncash expenses	1.952	2.326	2.633	2.756	
Decrease (increase) in					
net working capital (except cash)	2.026	0.423	(0.202)	(1.733)	
Net cash flow from operations	$7.192	$5.378	$4.533	$3.481	
Cash Flows from Investing Activities					
Fixed asset acquisitions	($4.722)	($6.402)	($7.687)	($4.327)	
Cash Flows from Financing Activities					
Increase (decrease) in long-term debt	($0.184)	($0.102)	$3.550	($1.428)	
Net increase (decrease) in cash	$2.286	($1.126)	$0.396	($2.274)	
Beginning cash and investments	$3.513	$5.799	$4.673	$5.069	
Ending cash and investments	$5.799	$4.673	$5.069	$2.795	

Note: The noncash expenses and fixed asset acquisitions data in the statements of cash flows are somewhat different than they would be if calculated directly from the other financial statements because of asset revaluations.

eight suits involving claims of various amounts that could ultimately be tried before juries. Although it is impossible to determine the exact potential liability in these claims, management does not believe that the settlement of these cases would have a material effect on the hospital's financial position.

Assume that you have just joined the staff of Eastside Memorial Hospital as assistant administrator. On your first day on the job, the administrator, Melissa Randolph, stated that the best way to get to know the financial and operating condition of the hospital is to do a thorough financial and operating analysis; thus, she assigned you the task. Although you also believe that a financial and operating analysis is a good

TABLE 1.4
Selected
Operating Data

	1998	1999	2000	2001	2002
Medicare discharges	3,008	2,960	2,721	2,860	2,741
Total discharges	9,680	9,311	8,784	8,318	8,576
Outpatient visits	30,754	31,960	32,285	32,878	36,796
Licensed beds	210	210	210	210	210
Staffed beds	192	196	193	197	178
Patient days	45,296	45,983	44,085	42,434	40,062
Case mix index	1.2531	1.2674	1.2869	1.2993	1.3161
Full-time equivalents	604.5	618.1	610.8	625.8	619.3

TABLE 1.5
Selected Industry
Financial Data

	2002 Industry Data (200–299 Beds)		
	+Quartile	Median	−Quartile
Profitability Ratios			
Deductible ratio*	0.34	0.26	0.18
Profit (total) margin	5.58%	3.48%	0.53%
Return on assets	5.80%	3.10%	0.40%
Return on equity	15.66%	6.01%	0.62%
Liquidity Ratios			
Current ratio	2.53	1.99	1.48
Days cash on hand	32.35	15.89	6.24
Debt Management Ratios			
Debt ratio	62.90%	48.40%	35.20%
Long-term debt to equity	127.00%	64.70%	26.90%
Times interest earned	4.29	2.23	1.14
Fixed charge coverage	2.18	1.35	1.02
Cash flow coverage	5.32	3.22	1.76
Asset Management Ratios			
Inventory turnover	98.68	63.95	43.99
Current asset turnover	3.94	3.38	2.88
Fixed asset turnover	2.20	1.76	1.49
Total asset turnover	1.04	0.89	0.75
Average collection period (days)	87.53	75.67	63.33
Average payment period (days)	71.24	56.52	45.84

	2002 Industry Data (200–299 Beds)		
	+Quartile	Median	–Quartile
Other Ratios			
Average age of plant (years)	8.86	7.39	6.14

TABLE 1.5
(continued)
Selected Industry
Financial Data

*Deductions/Gross patient service revenue

Notes: 1. The industry data shown here are for illustration purposes only and hence should not be used outside this case.

2. The upper quartile is based on the higher numerical value for the ratio and the lower quartile the lower numerical value, regardless of whether a high value is good or bad. The interpretation is left to the analyst.

	2002 Industry Data (200–299 Beds)		
	+Quartile	Median	–Quartile
Profit Indicators			
Profit per discharge[a]	$89.04	($21.30)	($120.08)
Profit per visit[b]	$ 6.22	$ 0.66	($ 7.01)
Net Price Indicators			
Net price per discharge	$4,091	$3,411	$ 2,815
Net price per visit	$ 201	$ 139	$ 98
Medicare payment percentage	43.47%	36.60%	31.25%
Bad debt/charity percentage[c]	7.89%	4.76%	2.97%
Contractual allowance%[d]	25.27%	20.02%	12.12%
Outpatient revenue%	25.26%	21.03%	17.44%
Volume Indicators			
Occupancy rate	67.12%	58.10%	47.84%
Average daily census[e]	173.23	144.73	114.39
Length of Stay Indicators			
Average length of stay (days)	6.80	6.07	5.41
Adjusted length of stay[f]	6.48	5.36	4.52

TABLE 1.6
Selected Industry
Operating Data

TABLE 1.6
(continued)
Selected Industry
Operating Data

	2002 Industry Data (200–299 Beds)		
	+Quartile	Median	–Quartile
Intensity of Service Indicators			
Cost per discharge	$ 3,937	$ 3,392	$ 2,972
Adjusted cost per discharge[g]	$ 3,417	$ 2,924	$ 2,572
Cost per visit[h]	$202.23	$141.97	$111.53
Case mix index	1.2795	1.1756	1.0259
Efficiency Indicators			
FTEs per occupied bed	4.59	4.15	3.77
Outpatient man-hours per visit[i]	4.68	5.84	8.66
Unit Cost Indicators			
Salary per FTE[j]	$24,447	$22,517	$20,347
Employee benefits percentage[k]	19.58%	17.04%	15.18%
Liability costs per discharge[l]	$ 80.94	$ 42.05	$ 18.31

[a](Net inpatient revenue – Inpatient cost)/Total discharges.
[b](Net outpatient revenue – Outpatient cost)/Total visits.
[c](Bad debt + Charity care)/Gross patient revenue.
[d]Contractual allowances/Gross patient revenue.
[e]Patient days/365.
[f]Average length of stay/Case mix index.
[g]Cost per discharge/Case mix index.
[h]Total outpatient expenses/Total outpatient visits.
[i](Outpatient FTEs x 2,080)/Total visits.
[j]Total salaries/FTEs.
[k]Fringe benefit costs/Total salaries.
[l]Inpatient professional liability costs/Total discharges.

Notes: 1. The industry data shown here are for illustration purposes only and hence should not be used outside this case.

2. The upper quartile is based on the higher numerical value for the ratio and the lower quartile the lower numerical value, regardless of whether a high value is good or bad. The interpretation is left to the analyst.

way to start, you wonder whether Melissa has any ulterior motives. Perhaps the hospital is having problems and she thinks that you can spot them or perhaps she wants to test your analytical skills. Melissa is from the "old school" of hospital management and has been looking for someone to bring modern management methods to the hospital.

In any event, she has already scheduled a financial performance analysis presentation for the next board of trustees meeting as a way for you to meet the board members. To help you structure your presentation, Melissa suggested that you make the following points:

1. Interpret the hospital's statements of cash flows.
2. Present an overview of the hospital's financial position using the Du Pont equation as a guide.
3. Use ratio analysis to identify the hospital's financial strengths and weaknesses.
4. Use operating analysis to identify the operational factors that explain the hospital's current financial condition.
5. Summarize your evaluation of the hospital's financial condition. However, *don't just rehash the numbers*; rather, present your views on the potential underlying economic and managerial factors that might have caused any problems that surfaced in the financial and operating analysis.
6. Finally, make any recommendations that you believe Eastside should follow to ensure future financial soundness.

In preparing for the presentation, several relevant factors came to light. First, in reviewing the policy decisions made by Eastside's board of trustees over the past decade, you noted that in 1997 the board made the decision to significantly expand the hospital's outpatient services. The rationale was that many procedures that historically were done on an inpatient basis were now being done in an outpatient setting, and if Eastside did not offer such services it would lose the patients to other providers. Furthermore, there was general agreement that outpatient services were more profitable than inpatient services.

Second, you discovered an AHA publication that identified six ratios that are believed to be "critical financial indicators." (For more information on the AHA, visit their web site at www.aha.org. Note in particular the studies and statistics that are available, especially those that provide financial benchmark information.) Table 1.7 provides information on the six critical financial indicators. You believe that using

**TABLE 1.7
AHA Critical
Financial
Indicators**

Cash Flow to Net Patient Service Revenue

Here, cash flow is defined as net income plus depreciation/amortization expense. The first line of the following comparative data gives the ratio values for four rating categories, while the second line gives the percentage of hospitals that fall into each category.

Very Poor	Poor	Good	Excellent
9.6% or less	9.6% to 12.3%	12.3% to 15.6%	15.6% or more
30.7%	25.3%	25.5%	18.5%

Cash Flow to Total Liabilities

Here, cash flow is defined as net income plus depreciation/amortization expense, and total liabilities represent everything on the right side of the balance sheet except equity.

Very Poor	Poor	Good	Excellent
15.8% or less	15.8% to 23.3%	23.3% to 32.4%	32.4% or more
31.4%	24.0%	22.6%	22.0%

Return to Total Revenue (Total Margin)

This ratio is net income divided by total revenues.

Very Poor	Poor	Good	Excellent
3.5% or less	3.5% to 6.0%	6.0% to 9.0%	9.0% or more
28.6%	26.7%	26.1%	18.6%

Return to Patient Service Revenue

This ratio is net income divided by net patient service revenue.

Very Poor	Poor	Good	Excellent
3.8% or less	3.8% to 6.3%	6.3% to 9.2%	9.2% or more
28.6%	26.7%	26.3%	18.4%

Case Mix Index

This value measures the general level of complexity of services offered. The theory is that a higher case mix index means better use of technology.

Very Poor	*Poor*	*Good*	*Excellent*
1.27 or less	1.27 to 1.42	1.42 to 1.65	1.65 or more
28.7%	27.5%	25.9%	17.9%

Age of Plant and Equipment

This measure (in years) is approximated by dividing accumulated depreciation by depreciation expense.

Very Poor	*Poor*	*Good*	*Excellent*
9.5 or more	8.1 to 9.5	7.1 to 8.1	7.1 or less
26.2%	29.6%	20.7%	23.5%

TABLE 1.7 (continued) AHA Critical Financial Indicators

some initiative in your presentation will impress the board, so you plan to include these indicators in your analysis and presentation.

Finally, the day before you make your presentation, Melissa catches you in the hallway. In addition to asking if you are ready to go, she asked whether or not management should be concerned about the hospital's annual economic value added (EVA) performance. Apparently, she just read an article in *Fortune* magazine that discusses this measure of managerial performance. (For more information on EVA, as well as market value added [MVA], see the Stern Stewart & Co. web site at www.eva.com.) As she was leaving for a meeting, she said, "By the way, our overall (corporate) cost of capital is 10 percent." You aren't quite sure why she passed that information on to you, but you jotted it down just in case.

PEACH STATE
HEALTH PLANS
ASSESSING HMO
PERFORMANCE

2

PEACH STATE HEALTH PLANS, INC., is one of Georgia's largest managed care organizations (MCOs). In fact, it is the largest of the state's not-for-profit MCOs. Peach State offers prepaid health coverage to more than 300,000 members in 15 counties, including the following major cities: Atlanta, Augusta, Columbus, Macon, and Savannah.

Peach State's various products include commercial health maintenance organizations (HMOs), preferred provider organizations (PPOs), and point of service (POS) plans as well as Medicare HMOs, which are all designed to meet the needs of a wide segment of Georgia's population of some 8 million. The breakdown of plan types is as follows:

Plan Type	Percent of Revenue
Commercial HMO	46
Medicare HMO	39
PPO	10
POS	5
	100

Peach State Health Plans was the first HMO in Georgia to seek and receive accreditation by the National Committee for Quality Assurance (NCQA), and each of its component plans have the highest accreditation level: Excellent. NCQA judges HMOs on how well they comply with more than 60 standards and performance measures that fall into five broad categories: access and service, qualified providers, staying healthy, getting better, and living with illness. Some of the evaluation focuses on systems and processes, but accreditation results also depend on clinical performance as measured by HEDIS (Health Plan Employer Data and Information Set). (For more information on the NCQA and HEDIS, visit the NCQA web site at www.ncqa.org.)

A summary of Peach State's 2001 and 2002 HMO plan financial data is presented in Table 2.1, while Table 2.2 contains a summary of operating and enrollment data. To help in analyzing Peach State's performance, its managers have classified the following four Georgia HMOs as "primary competitors."

HMO	Number of Counties Served	2002 Total Enrollment	2002 Total Assets (000s)
WellLife	23	516,858	$408,707
Signet Healthcare	15	360,252	178,662
Proxima	15	247,109	144,982
Sparta	28	205,296	103,504

These plans have the geographical coverage and financial resources to be permanent players in the Georgia managed care industry. Furthermore, the primary competitors are operating in the same service areas and have a similar product mix as Peach State and hence are potential threats to its future success. In addition to comparisons to national data, all internal analyses that use benchmarking compare Peach State's performance to the state average as well as to the primary competitor list. Note, however, that not all relevant performance measures have a complete set of comparative data available.

Table 2.3 contains selected financial and operating ratios for Peach State's primary competitors as well as the means and medians for all Georgia HMOs. Table 2.4 contains selected national data. Note that all comparative data are for HMO plans only. Data relevant to competitors' other plans, such as PPO and POS plans, are not available. (For a better understanding of the types of comparative data available for managed care plans, see the InterStudy Publications web site at www.hmodata.com.) Table 2.5 contains selected ratio definitions.

Assume that you have just started an administrative residency at Peach State Health Plans. On your first day at the organization, Charles

	2001	2002
Statements of Operations		
Premium revenue	$313.7	$357.6
Interest income	2.4	3.5
Total revenues	$316.1	$361.1
Operating expenses:		
Medical costs	$263.0	$291.8
Selling and administrative	36.8	43.6
Depreciation	4.7	5.0
Total operating expenses	$304.5	$340.4
Net income	$ 11.6	$ 20.7
Balance Sheets		
Cash	$ 37.2	$ 27.2
Marketable securities	42.7	60.9
Premiums receivable	3.7	7.4
Total current assets	$ 83.6	$ 95.5
Net fixed assets	30.0	31.7
Total assets	$113.6	$127.2
Medical costs payable	$ 44.8	$ 48.7
Trade accounts payable/accruals	15.4	17.3
Total current liabilities	$ 60.2	$ 66.0
Long-term debt	17.1	4.2
Net assets	36.3	57.0
Total liabilities and net assets	$113.6	$127.2
Other Data		
Total commercial premium revenue	$170.9	$205.6
Total Medicare revenue	$142.8	$152.0
Total physician services expense	$125.6	$127.1
Total inpatient expense	$ 80.8	$ 90.1
Total other medical expense	$ 56.6	$ 74.6

TABLE 2.1
Peach State Health Plans:
HMO Plan Financial Data
(millions of dollars)

TABLE 2.2
Peach State Health Plans:
HMO Plan Operating
and Enrollment Data

	2001	2002
Commercial premium revenue PMPM	$127.82	$127.90
Medicare revenue PMPM	$449.37	$437.23
Commercial patient days per 1,000 enrollees	302.9	266.4
Medicare patient days per 1,000 enrollees	1,622.4	1,418.1
Commercial member–months	1,337,036	1,607,036
Commercial physician encounters	594,381	622,749
Commercial inpatient days	43,661	39,763
Medicare member–months	317,778	347,643
Medicare physician encounters	149,622	185,283
Medicare inpatient days	28,416	26,736

TABLE 2.3
Selected State HMO
Industry Financial and
Operating Data
(millions of dollars)

	2001	2002
Total Margin		
WellLife	4.8%	5.8%
Signet Healthcare	3.0	3.2
Proxima	9.1	(0.7)
Sparta	10.5	9.1
Georgia average	3.8	(3.9)
Georgia median	4.8	4.7
Percent Administrative Expense		
WellLife	12.1%	11.5%
Signet Healthcare	12.2	13.4
Proxima	13.6	16.4
Sparta	23.9	26.8
Georgia average	15.5	17.4
Georgia median	14.8	15.7

	2001	*2002*
Percent Inpatient Expense		
WellLife	32.2%	30.3%
Signet Healthcare	22.8	22.4
Proxima	21.2	23.0
Sparta	18.2	18.8
Georgia average	25.2	23.3
Georgia median	23.6	24.3
Percent Physician Expense		
WellLife	54.1%	56.9%
Signet Healthcare	31.3	30.3
Proxima	22.7	24.9
Sparta	12.8	18.6
Georgia average	28.8	31.3
Georgia median	31.1	31.6
Percent Other Medical Expense		
WellLife	0.1%	0.1%
Signet Healthcare	8.9	7.8
Proxima	27.5	30.2
Sparta	45.7	35.0
Georgia average	14.6	12.5
Georgia median	10.2	8.9
Commercial Premium Revenue PMPM		
WellLife	$108.68	$110.19
Signet Healthcare	39.86	27.50
Proxima	120.68	124.27
Sparta	88.41	95.06
Georgia average	101.17	102.53
Georgia median	108.32	108.95

TABLE 2.3
(continued)
Selected State HMO Industry Financial and Operating Data
(millions of dollars)

TABLE 2.3
(continued)
Selected State HMO
Industry Financial and
Operating Data
(millions of dollars)

	2001	2002
Medicare Revenue PMPM		
WellLife	$406.57	$421.57
Signet Healthcare	N/A	N/A
Proxima	N/A	N/A
Sparta	N/A	N/A
Georgia average	365.12	376.04
Georgia median	426.18	430.57
Commercial Inpatient Days per 1,000 Enrollees		
WellLife	245.4	246.0
Signet Healthcare	258.4	248.8
Proxima	251.8	259.2
Sparta	198.2	248.9
Georgia average	278.0	237.0
Georgia median	279.1	248.8
Medicare Inpatient Days per 1,000 Enrollees		
WellLife	1,388.4	1,323.8
Signet Healthcare	1,165.2	1,188.7
Proxima	1,518.8	1,382.2
Sparta	1,623.8	1,566.9
Georgia average	1,432.1	1,375.5
Georgia median	1,380.5	1,350.6
Commercial Physician Encounters per Member		
WellLife	2.2	3.6
Signet Healthcare	1.5	1.4
Proxima	2.7	2.6
Sparta	3.5	3.6
Georgia average	3.8	3.8
Georgia median	3.9	3.7

	2001	2002
Medicare Physician Encounters per Member		
WellLife	9.8	9.6
Signet Healthcare	6.6	6.9
Proxima	10.1	10.0
Sparta	11.2	11.3
Georgia average	9.1	9.1
Georgia median	8.6	8.9

Note: The Georgia data for the HMO industry contained in this table are for illustrative purposes only. These data should not be used to conduct actual financial analyses.

TABLE 2.3 (continued)
Selected State HMO Industry Financial and Operating Data (millions of dollars)

Average copay per office visit	$ 8
Average copay per hospitalization	$36
Average copay per pharmacy prescription	$ 7
Medical loss ratio:	
Upper quartile	89.0%
Median	84.9
Lower quartile	80.0
Administrative cost ratio:	
Upper quartile	14.4%
Median	12.0
Lower quartile	9.0
Operating margin:	
Upper quartile	5.0%
Median	2.5
Lower quartile	1.1
Total margin:	
Upper quartile	5.5%
Median	2.9
Lower quartile	1.5

TABLE 2.4
Selected 2002 National HMO Industry Financial and Operating Data

Return on assets (ROA):	
Upper quartile	16.5%
Median	11.3
Lower quartile	4.8
Return on equity (ROE):	
Upper quartile	50.2%
Median	31.4
Lower quartile	18.2
Current ratio:	
Upper quartile	1.29
Median	0.95
Lower quartile	0.49
Days cash on hand:	
Upper quartile	32.7
Median	10.3
Lower quartile	0.8
Current asset turnover:	
Upper quartile	14.1
Median	6.4
Lower quartile	3.7
Total asset turnover:	
Upper quartile	4.1
Median	3.1
Lower quartile	2.2
Days premiums receivable:	
Upper quartile	14.0
Median	8.9
Lower quartile	7.0
Debt ratio:	
Upper quartile	81.3%
Median	68.4
Lower quartile	59.7

Note: The national data for the HMO industry contained in this table are for illustrative purposes only. These data should not be used to conduct actual financial analyses.

TABLE 2.5
Selected Ratio
Definitions

Medical Loss Ratio

$$\frac{\text{Medical expenses}}{\text{Premium revenue}}$$

Administrative Cost Ratio

$$\frac{\text{Selling and administrative expenses + Depreciation}}{\text{Premium revenue}}$$

Operating Margin

$$\frac{\text{Net income − Interest income}}{\text{Premium revenue}}$$

Percent Administrative Expense

$$\frac{\text{Selling and administrative expense}}{\text{Total operating expenses}}$$

Percent Inpatient Expense

$$\frac{\text{Inpatient expense}}{\text{Total operating expenses}}$$

Percent Physician Expense

$$\frac{\text{Physician services expense}}{\text{Total operating expenses}}$$

Percent Other Medical Expense

$$\frac{\text{Other medical expense}}{\text{Total operating expenses}}$$

Redman, the CEO, stated that the best way to get to know the financial and operating condition of any business is to do a brief financial and operating analysis; thus, he assigned you the task. Although you also believe that a financial and operating analysis is a good way to start, you wonder whether he has any hidden motives. Perhaps the company is having financial problems and he thinks that you can spot them or perhaps he just wants to test your analytical skills.

In any event, he has already scheduled a financial/operating analysis presentation for the next executive committee meeting as a way for you to demonstrate your skills to Peach State's senior managers. In preparing for the meeting, you call Jennifer Wall, the previous administrative resident, to get some hints on what to prepare for the executive committee. Jennifer just left Peach State for a high-paying job with Humana. Her advice was to just do a standard financial statement analysis. "Oh by the way," she said, "you had better create a statement of

TABLE 2.6
Statement of Cash
Flows Outline

Cash Flows from Operating Activities
  Income from operations
  Depreciation
  Increase in premiums receivable
  Increase in medical costs payable
  Increase in payables/accruals

    Net cash flow from operations

Cash Flows from Investing Activities
  Fixed asset acquisitions

Cash Flows from Financing Activities
  Reduction in long-term debt
  Increase in marketable securities

    Net cash flow from financing

Net increase (decrease) in cash

Beginning cash

Ending cash

cash flows for 2002." She went on to say that Mr. Redman always holds that statement back, but he expects the resident to be able to create one based on the income statements and balance sheets provided. As you consider this task, you create the outline for the statement shown in Table 2.6. Creation and interpretation of that statement seem to be part of the "initiation rite." As you were hanging up, she said, "Don't forget to do a Du Pont analysis."

As you began the analysis, it became apparent that the ratios used and their interpretations differ across industries; that is, the ratios that are critical to identifying a hospital's financial condition are not necessarily the same as the ratios critical to a managed care plan. To help the executive committee in their interpretation of your presentation, you plan to point out key differences between your analysis and that for a hospital as they occur.

Managerial Accounting

MARICOPA HEALTHCARE EISENHOWER

3

COST ALLOCATION
CONCEPTS

MARICOPA HEALTHCARE EISENHOWER is a full-service not-for-profit acute care hospital with 325 beds located in Scottsdale, Arizona. It is part of the three-hospital Maricopa Healthcare System. The bulk of the hospital's facilities are devoted to inpatient care and emergency services. However, a 100,000 square foot section of the hospital complex is devoted to outpatient services. Currently, this space has two primary uses. About 80 percent of the space is used by the Outpatient Clinic, which handles all routine outpatient services offered by the hospital. The remaining 20 percent is used by the Dialysis Center.

The Dialysis Center performs hemodialysis and peritoneal dialysis, which are alternative processes that remove wastes and excess water from the blood for patients with end-stage renal (kidney) disease. In hemodialysis, blood is pumped from the patient's arm through a shunt into a dialysis machine, which uses a cleansing solution and an artificial membrane to perform the functions of a healthy kidney. Then, the cleansed blood is pumped back into the patient through a second shunt. In peritoneal dialysis, the cleansing solution is inserted directly into the abdominal cavity through a catheter. The body naturally cleanses the blood through the peritoneum—a thin membrane that lines the abdominal cavity. In general, hemodialysis patients require three dialyses a week, with each treatment lasting about four hours. Patients who use peritoneal dialysis change their own cleansing solutions at home, typically four times a day. However, the patient's overall condition, as well as the positioning of the catheter, must be monitored regularly at the Dialysis Center.

Maricopa's new cost accounting system, which was installed two years ago, allocates facilities costs (which at Maricopa consist essentially of building depreciation and interest on long-term debt) on the basis of square footage. Currently, the facilities cost allocation rate is $15 per square foot, so the facilities cost allocation is 20,000 × $15 = $300,000 for the Dialysis Center and 80,000 × $15 = $1,200,000 for the Outpatient Clinic. All other overhead costs, such as administration, finance, maintenance, and housekeeping, are lumped together and called "general overhead." These costs are allocated on the basis of 10 percent of the revenues of each patient service department. The current allocation of general overhead is $270,000 for the Dialysis Center and $1,600,000 for the Outpatient Clinic, which result in total overhead allocations of $570,000 for the Dialysis Center and $2,800,000 for the Outpatient Clinic.

Recent growth in utilization of the Outpatient Clinic has created a need for 25 percent more space than currently assigned. Because the Outpatient Clinic is much larger than the Dialysis Center, and because its patients need frequent access to other departments within the hospital, the decision was made to keep the Outpatient Clinic in its current location and to move the Dialysis Center to another location to free up space within the hospital complex. Such a move would give the Outpatient Clinic 100,000 square feet, a 25 percent increase.

After attempting to find space for the Dialysis Center within the hospital complex, it was soon determined that a new 20,000 square foot building must be built. This building would be situated two blocks away from the hospital complex, in a location that would be much more convenient for dialysis patients because of ease of parking. The 20,000 square feet of space, which could be more efficiently utilized than the old space, allows for some increase in patient volume, although it is unclear whether or not the move will generate additional dialysis patients.

Cost of the new building is estimated at $120 per square foot, for a total cost of $2,400,000. Additionally, furniture and other fittings, along with relocation of equipment, files, and other items, would cost $1,600,000, for a total cost of $4,000,000. The $4,000,000 cost would be financed by a 7.75 percent, 20-year first mortgage loan. When both

Revenues		
Hemodialysis program	$ 1,300,000	
Peritoneal dialysis program	600,000	
Medical (pharmacy) supplies	800,000	
Total revenues	$ 2,700,000	
Direct Expenses		
Salaries and benefits	$ 900,000	
Pharmacy purchases	800,000	
Other medical/administrative supplies	100,000	
Utilities	80,000	
Lease expense	120,000	
Other expenses	100,000	
Total expenses	$ 2,100,000	
Net gain (loss) before indirect costs	$ 600,000	
Indirect Expenses		
Facilities costs	$ 300,000	
General overhead	270,000	
Total overhead costs	$ 570,000	
Net profit	$ 30,000	

TABLE 3.1
Dialysis Center: Pro Forma P&L Statement Assuming Status Quo

Notes: 1. Revenues from hemodialysis are based on the Medicare rate of $110 per treatment.
2. Revenues from peritoneal dialysis are based on the Medicare rate of $47 per treatment.

the principal amount (which can be considered depreciation) and interest are amortized over 20 years, the end result is an annual cost of financing of $400,000. Thus, it is possible to estimate the actual annual facilities costs for the new Dialysis Center, something that is rarely possible for other units in the hospital.

Table 3.1 contains the projected profit and loss (P&L) statement for the Dialysis Center before adjusting for the move. Maricopa's department heads receive annual bonuses on the basis of each department's

contribution to the hospital's bottom line (profit). In the past, only direct costs were considered, but Maricopa's CEO has decided that bonuses would now be based on full (total) costs. Obviously, the new
approach to awarding bonuses, coupled with the potential for increases
in indirect cost allocation, is of great concern to John Van Pelt, the
director of the Dialysis Center. Under the current (Table 3.1) allocation
of indirect costs, John would have a reasonable chance at an end-of-
year bonus, as the forecast puts the Dialysis Center "in the black." However, any increase in the indirect cost allocation would likely put him
"out of the money."

At the next department heads' meeting, John voiced his concern
about the impact of any allocation changes on the Dialysis Center's
profitability, so Maricopa's CEO asked the CFO, Rick Simmons, to
look into the matter. In essence, the CEO said that the final allocation
is up to Rick, but that any allocation changes must be made within
outpatient services. In other words, any change in indirect cost allocation to the Dialysis Center must be offset by an equal, but opposite,
change in the allocation to the Outpatient Clinic.

To get started, Rick created Table 3.2. The new Dialysis Center
would have the same number of stations as the old one, the same patients would be served, and the reimbursement rates would remain
unchanged. Also, direct operating expenses would differ only slightly
from the current situation because the same personnel and equipment
would be used. Thus, for all practical purposes, the revenues and direct
costs of the Dialysis Center would be unaffected by the move.

The data in Table 3.2 for the expanded Outpatient Clinic are based
on the assumption that the expansion would allow utilization to increase by 25 percent and that both revenues and direct costs would increase by a like amount. Furthermore, to keep the analysis manageable,
the assumption was made that the overall hospital allocation rates for
both facilities costs and general overhead would not materially change
because of the expansion.

Rick knew that his "trial balloon" allocation, which is shown in
Table 3.2 in the columns labeled "Initial Allocation," would create some
controversy. In the past, facilities costs were aggregated, so all departments were charged a cost based on the average embedded (historical)
cost regardless of the actual age (or value) of the space occupied. Thus,
a basement room with no windows was allocated the same facilities
costs (per square foot) as was the fifth floor executive suite. Because

TABLE 3.2
Dialysis Center (DC) and Outpatient Clinic (OC) Summary Projections

P&L Statements:

| | Without Expansion | | With Expansion | | | |
| | | | Initial Allocation | | Alternative Allocation | |
	DC	OC	DC	OC	DC	OC
Revenues/Direct Costs						
Total revenues	$ 2,700,000	$16,000,000	$ 2,700,000	$20,000,000	$ 2,700,000	$20,000,000
Direct expenses	2,100,000	9,833,155	2,100,000	12,291,444	2,100,000	12,291,444
Contribution margin	$ 600,000	$ 6,166,845	$ 600,000	$ 7,708,556	$ 600,000	$ 7,708,556
Percent of revenues	22.2%	38.5%	22.2%	38.5%	22.2%	38.5%
Indirect Costs						
Facilities costs	$ 300,000	$ 1,200,000	$ 400,000	$ 1,500,000	$	$
General overhead	270,000	1,600,000	270,000	2,000,000		
Total overhead	$ 570,000	$ 2,800,000	$ 670,000	$ 3,500,000	$	$
Net profit	$ 30,000	$ 3,366,845	($ 70,000)	$ 4,208,556	$	$
Percent of revenues	1.1%	21.0%	(2.6%)	21.0%	%	%
Facilities Cost Allocation:						
Square footage	20,000	80,000	20,000	100,000	20,000	100,000
Facilities costs per square foot	$ 15.00	$ 15.00	$ 20.00	$ 15.00	$	$
Other Overhead Allocation:						
General overhead costs as a % of revenue	10.0%	10.0%	10.0%	10.0%	%	%

Note: The term "contribution margin" as used here means the amount available to cover overhead costs as opposed to the more traditional meaning of the amount available to cover fixed costs.

many department heads thought this approach to be unfair, Rick wanted to begin allocating facilities overhead on a true cost basis. Thus, in his initial allocation, Rick used actual facilities costs as the basis for the allocation to the Dialysis Center.

Needless to say, John's response to the initial allocation was less than enthusiastic. Specifically, he raised these points:

1. Is it fair for the Dialysis Center to suffer (in profitability) from the move even though it had nothing to do with it?

2. Should the Dialysis Center be charged actual facilities costs for its new location? After all, the move was forced by the Outpatient Clinic, which is being charged for facilities at the lower average allocation rate. Under the concept of charging for actual facilities costs, department heads might be better off by resisting proposed moves to new (and potentially more efficient) facilities because such moves would result in increased facilities allocations.

3. Even if the true cost concept were applied to the Dialysis Center, is the $400,000 annual allocation amount correct? After all, the building has a useful life that is probably significantly longer than 20 years—the life of the loan used to determine the allocation amount.

4. It appears that the revenue that the Dialysis Center "receives" from patient use of the pharmacy is passed on directly to the pharmacy. Should this "revenue" be counted when general overhead allocations are made?

Before Rick was able to respond to John's concerns, he suddenly left Maricopa to be the CFO of a competing investor-owned hospital. The task of completing the allocation study was given to you, Maricopa's current administrative resident. You remember that to be of most benefit to the organization, cost allocation should (1) be perceived as being fair by the parties involved and (2) promote overall cost savings within the organization. However, you also realize that in practice cost allocation is very complex and somewhat arbitrary. Perhaps the best approach to overhead allocations is what might be called the "Marxist approach," by which allocations are based on each patient service department's ability to cover overhead costs. But this approach also has its disadvantages.

Considering all the relevant issues, you must develop and justify a new indirect cost allocation scheme for outpatient services. Summarize your results in the "Alternative Allocation" columns of Table 3.2 and be prepared to justify your recommendations at the next department heads' meeting.

TWIN CITIES FAMILY PRACTICE

COST ALLOCATION METHODS

4

TWIN CITIES FAMILY PRACTICE (the Group) is a group practice with four locations in the Minneapolis and St. Paul area. The clinical staff consists of 20 physicians, all of whom practice in one or more areas of family medicine, and 33 nurses. The Group is organized into three patient services departments: Adult Medicine, Obstetrics, and Pediatrics. To support these patient services departments, the practice has three support departments: Administration, Facilities, and Finance. Table 4.1 contains the Group's summary revenue and cost projections by department for the coming year.

As part of a much-needed overhaul of the cost allocation process, the Group contracted with a major accounting firm to estimate the amount of services provided by the support departments to each other and to each patient service department. The intent of the study was to provide data that would help the Group develop a better cost allocation system than the outdated, arbitrary system currently in use. The results of this study are contained in Table 4.2. Although expressed as percentages of the total dollar amount of support provided to other departments (instead of the more typical cost allocation rates), the data in Table 4.2 are based on an extensive study using sound managerial accounting techniques. Thus, both senior management and department heads at the Group are comfortable with the resulting allocation percentages. (Hint: To ensure that you apply the percentages properly, be sure to pay attention to Note 2 at the bottom of Table 4.2.)

TABLE 4.1		
Twin Cities	*Revenues*	
Family Practice:	Adult Medicine	$12,000,000
Departmental Revenue	Obstetrics	6,000,000
and Cost Projections	Pediatrics	2,000,000
	Total revenues	$20,000,000
	Direct Costs	
	Patient Services	
	Adult Medicine	$ 6,000,000
	Obstetrics	3,600,000
	Pediatrics	1,200,000
	Subtotal	$10,800,000
	Support	
	Administration	1,000,000
	Facilities	4,400,000
	Finance	1,800,000
	Subtotal	$ 7,200,000
	Total expenses	$18,000,000
	Pre-tax profit	$ 2,000,000

The second step in the cost allocation process improvement initiative is to choose the allocation method. There are four allocation methods under consideration: direct, step-down, double apportionment, and reciprocal. To aid in the decision, George Poulis, The Group's vice president of finance, has asked Mary Jansen, a resident temporarily assigned to the finance department, to conduct a study and to make a recommendation regarding the best method for the Group.

There are several possible approaches to the task, but Mary has decided to "examine by doing"—that is, she plans to use the data in Tables 4.1 and 4.2 to determine the overhead cost allocations under each method. Once this is done, she will be able to compare and contrast the results. Of course, the final decision cannot be made without considering the costs involved in implementing each allocation method. When Mary asked George about the costs inherent in each allocation method, George said, "Hell, I don't know! Assume that the direct method is the least costly, the reciprocal method is the most costly, and the

	Percentage of Services Provided by			
Services Provided to	Administration	Facilities	Finance
Administration	—	5%	5%
Facilities	10%	—	5
Finance	10	10	—
Adult Medicine	35	55	50
Obstetrics	20	10	25
Pediatrics	25	20	15
Total	100%	100%	100%
Percentage to Support Departments	20%	15%	10%
Percentage to Patient Services	80%	85%	90%

TABLE 4.2
Twin Cities
Family Practice:
Allocation Percentages

Notes: 1. The allocation percentages are based on a two-year analysis of the actual services provided by the support departments to other departments.

2. To use the percentages to perform an allocation, they may have to be adjusted to ensure that the entire amount of the cost pool is allocated. To illustrate, in the direct method, all of the Administration Department's costs ($500,000) have to be allocated directly in a single allocation to the three patient service departments. If the raw percentages were used, only 35% + 20% + 25% = 80% of the cost pool would be allocated. Thus, the allocation percentages have to be adjusted so that 80 percent represents the entire allocation (100 percent). This is done by adjusting the raw percentages as follows. First, note that the patient service allocations sum to 80 percent. Thus, instead of a 35 percent allocation to Adult Medicine, its adjusted allocation is 35% / 80% = 43.75%. In a similar manner, the adjusted allocation to Obstetrics is 20% / 80% = 25%, while the adjusted allocation to Pediatrics is 25%/ 80% = 31.25%. When done correctly, the adjusted percentages must sum to 100%: 43.75% + 25% + 31.25% = 100%.

other two fall somewhere in between." He also said that he expects Mary to make some judgments on the relative profitability of the patient services departments under the recommended allocation system.

Mary began her analysis by reviewing the allocation methods presented in her old healthcare finance textbook. She had no problem remembering basic cost allocation concepts, but she did hit two snags.

First, the textbook did not describe the double apportionment method. However, after a little research, Mary discovered that the double apportionment method is a slightly more complicated version of the step-down method. In essence, the double apportionment method first recognizes support provided by service departments to all other service departments as well as to the patient services departments. After this step, which is called the first allocation (apportionment), some costs still remain in the support departments. Then, a second apportionment, which uses the step-down method, is used to move all remaining support department costs to the patient services departments. In this method, service department support to all other service departments is recognized, while in the pure step-down method, service department support is recognized only to "downstream" service departments.

Here's how Mary assumed that the double apportionment method would be applied to the Group. (There are alternative ways in which this allocation method can be applied.) First, the direct Administration costs would be allocated to the other five departments (two support and three patient services). Second, direct Facilities costs would be allocated to all other departments (including Administration and Finance). Third, direct Finance costs would be allocated to all other departments (including Administration and Facilities). After these three allocations are completed, the first apportionment is finished. Some costs still remain in the support departments—the intra-support department allocations from the first apportionment—so a second apportionment is necessary. The second apportionment is conducted using the step-down method as it is normally applied, except that the application of the first apportionment means that the starting cost pool values are much lower.

The second problem Mary faced was how to perform the reciprocal allocation. One method is to use simultaneous equations, but higher mathematics has never been Mary's strong suit, while the second method uses an iterative approach. Fortunately, Mary read an article in *Accounting Monthly* that included an Excel® model that uses the iterative approach to accomplish reciprocal allocation. To help with the analysis, Mary created a new spreadsheet model, which uses the Group's numbers, to calculate the allocation not only for the reciprocal method but also for the other three methods.

Assume that you are in Mary's shoes. Complete her assignment and prepare a report to present to the Group's executive committee. In addition to merely completing the task as it stands, you decide to assess

Sensitivity to Changes in Relative Overhead Costs:

New Direct Expenses for Calculation 1

Administration	$4,400,000
Facilities	1,000,000
Finance	1,800,000
Total overhead expenses	$7,200,000

New Direct Expenses for Calculation 2

Administration	$1,000,000
Facilities	1,800,000
Finance	4,400,000
Total overhead expenses	$7,200,000

Sensitivity to Allocation Percentages:

Services Provided To	*Percentage of Services Provided By*		
	Administration	*Facilities*	*Finance*
Administration	—	25%	20%
Facilities	30%	—	20
Finance	30	25	—
Adult Medicine	18	32	33
Obstetrics	10	6	17
Pediatrics	12	12	10
Total	100%	100%	100%
Percentage to Support Departments	60%	50%	40%
Percentage to Patient Services	40%	50%	60%

TABLE 4.3
Twin Cities
Family Practice:
Sensitivity Analysis
Values

the sensitivity of the results to (1) the relative sizes of the direct costs at each support department and (2) the amount of support provided by the support departments to each other. Table 4.3 contains the values that you intend to use in your sensitivity analysis.

NEW ENGLAND HMO
PREMIUM DEVELOPMENT

5

NEW ENGLAND HMO, a regional not-for-profit managed care company headquartered in Boston, currently has over 500,000 enrollees in 25 different plans in Connecticut, Maine, Massachusetts, New Hampshire, Rhode Island, and Vermont. It has recently been contacted by a consortium of employers, including such major companies as IBM, Ford, and Prudential Insurance, regarding its interest in bidding on a managed care (HMO) contract to be offered to the consortium's 75,000 employees located in and around Nashua, New Hampshire.

New England's approach to premium development starts with the recognition that the premium received from employers must cover two different categories of expenses: (1) the cost of providing required healthcare services (medical costs) and (2) the costs of administering the plan and of establishing reserves (other costs). Reserves, which typically are required by state insurance regulators, are necessary to ensure that funds are available to pay providers when medical costs exceed the amount collected in premium payments. New England, as a not-for-profit corporation, does not explicitly include a profit element in its premium. However, the reserve requirement is set sufficiently high so that income from reserve investments is available to fund product expansion and growth, so, in effect, a portion of the reserve requirement constitutes profit.

New England uses a multistep approach in setting its premiums. First, a base per member per month (PMPM) cost is estimated for each

41

of the plan's covered benefits. When the premiums are initially established for a new subscriber group, the base PMPM costs are usually developed on the basis of historical utilization and cost data. If data are available on the specific subscriber group, as with the consortium contract, these data are used. Otherwise, the base PMPM costs are based on utilization and cost data from one or more proxy groups, which are chosen to match as closely as possible the demographic, utilization, and cost patterns that will be experienced with the new contract. Also, any utilization or cost savings that will result from New England's aggressive utilization management program should be factored into the premium.

The base PMPM costs then are adjusted to reflect the dollar amount of copayments to providers as well as the estimated impact of copayment and benefit options on utilization and hence medical costs. Copayments, which are an additional source of revenue to the provider panel, reduce New England's medical costs and thus lower the consortium's premium. Furthermore, the higher the copayment, the lower the utilization of that service, especially if it is noncritical. Finally, the more restrictive the benefits package, the lower the costs associated with medical services. The end result, after these adjustments are made, is an adjusted PMPM cost for each service, which are then summed to obtain the total medical PMPM amount.

To estimate the total nonmedical PMPM amount, New England typically adds 15 percent to the total medical PMPM amount for administrative costs and 5 percent for reserves. The sum of the total medical and total nonmedical amounts, which is called the "total PMPM amount," is the per member amount that New England must collect from the consortium each month to meet the total costs of serving the healthcare needs of its employees—the subscribers to the plan.

Once the total PMPM amount is calculated, it must be converted into actual premium rates for individuals and families. Using data provided by the consortium, New England estimates that 45 percent of subscribers will elect individual coverage, while the remaining 55 percent will choose family coverage. New England plans to offer the consortium a two-rate structure, under which employees may elect either single or family coverage. Data from the consortium indicate that family coverage, on average, includes 3.5 individuals, so, all else the same, the premiums for families should be 3.5 times as much as for individuals. However, children typically consume less healthcare services, on a dollar basis, than do adults, so final premiums must reflect such differentials.

Table 5.1 contains a partially completed copy of the worksheet that New England uses to establish its final premium on any contract. The worksheet provides a relatively easy guide for implementing the procedures described above. Table 5.2 contains the relevant cost and utilization adjustment factors for a variety of service and copayment options. Once the decision has been made on the appropriate service and copay structure, these adjustment factors feed into the calculations in Table 5.1 for each service's medical PMPM amount.

Table 5.3 contains the factors required to obtain individual and family premium rates. In setting the specific premium rates, New England must make sure that the total premiums paid, which are not all paid by single (individual) members, equal the estimated total premiums to be collected based on the estimated PMPM rate. The 75,000 population that would be served by the contract consists (roughly) of 12,000 individual members and 18,000 families. Thus, 75,000 × Total PMPM amount must equal (12,000 × Single premium) + (18,000 × Family premium).

The consortium has furnished New England with a significant amount of data concerning its employees' current utilization of healthcare services. Table 5.4 contains inpatient cost and utilization data. Note, however, that a recent survey of New Hampshire hospitals indicates that most managed care contracts call for per diem payments in the range of $800 to $1,000. Additionally, New England's experience with similar employee groups indicates that moderate utilization management would result in 300–350 inpatient days per 1,000 plan members.

Table 5.5 contains current cost and utilization data for other facility services including skilled nursing care, inpatient mental health care, hospital surgical services, and emergency room care. Table 5.6 contains data on primary care services, while Table 5.7 focuses on specialist office visits.

Note that the total PMPM amount shown in Table 5.1 may be modified to reflect anticipated medical cost inflation. This adjustment is especially critical if the total PMPM premium is based on relatively old cost data. For the most part, the cost data provided in the case can be assumed to be two years old. (Although the data is for last year, the contract would not be in place for yet another year.)

TABLE 5.1
New England HMO: Premium Development Worksheet

I. Medical Expenses

	Base PMPM Cost	Copay Adjustment Factors		Adjusted PMPM
		Cost	Utilization	
Facility Services				
Inpatient:				
Acute	$			$
Skilled nursing				
Mental health				
Substance abuse	0.41	1.0000	1.0000	0.41
Surgical procedures				
Emergency room				
Outpatient procedures	3.43	1.0000	1.0000	3.43
Total facilities				———
Physician Services				
Primary care services				
Specialist services:				
Office visits				
Surgical services	9.00	0.9544	1.0000	8.59
All other services	23.67	0.8659	0.9100	18.65
Total physicians				———
Total medical PMPM amount				———

II. Nonmedical Expenses

Administrative
Reserves

Total nonmedical PMPM amount   ═══════

III. Total Expenses

Total PMPM amount

IV. Premium Rates

	Single	Family
Rate factor	———	———
Premium rate	═══════	═══════

	Patient Copay Amount	Copay Cost Adj Factor	Copay Utilization Adj Factor	
Facility Services				
Inpatient acute	$ 0	1.0000	1.0000	
	100	0.9851	0.9750	
	150	0.9777	0.9600	
	250	0.9642	0.9200	
Skilled nursing	$ 0	1.0000	1.0000	
Mental health:				
30-day limit	$ 0	1.0000	0.9524	
	100	0.9805	0.9286	
	150	0.9707	0.9143	
	250	0.9532	0.8762	
60-day limit	$ 0	1.0000	1.2000	
	100	0.9845	1.1700	
	150	0.9768	1.1520	
	250	0.9628	1.1040	
90-day limit	$ 0	1.0000	1.2500	
	100	0.9851	1.2188	
	150	0.9777	1.2000	
	250	0.9643	1.1500	
Surgical procedures	$ 0	1.0000	1.0000	
	100	0.9231	1.0000	
	150	0.8846	1.0000	
	250	0.8077	1.0000	
Emergency room	$ 0	1.0857	1.0250	
	15	1.0000	1.0000	
	25	0.9429	0.9850	
	50	0.8000	0.9550	

TABLE 5.2
New England HMO: Cost and Utilization Adjustment Factors

TABLE 5.2
(continued)
New England HMO:
Cost and Utilization
Adjustment Factors

	Patient Copay Amount	Copay Cost Adj Factor	Copay Utilization Adj Factor
Primary Care Services	$ 0	1.0352	1.0150
	5	1.0000	1.0000
	10	0.9472	0.9800
	15	0.8593	0.9500
	20	0.7713	0.9200
	25	0.6834	0.8900
Specialist Services			
Zero PCP Copay	$ 0	1.0000	1.0000
	5	0.8897	0.9730
	10	0.7795	0.9590
	15	0.6692	0.9450
$10 PCP Copay	$ 0	1.0000	0.9920
	5	0.8897	0.9600
	10	0.7795	0.9460
	15	0.6692	0.9320
$20 PCP Copay	$ 0	1.0000	0.9680
	5	0.8897	0.9360
	10	0.7795	0.9220
	15	0.6692	0.9080

Note: New England uses various incentive systems to control utilization of specialty services. One system requires primary care physicians (PCPs) to copay for each specialist office visit.

TABLE 5.3
New England HMO:
Individual and
Family Rate Factors

	Two Rate Structures	
	Single	Family
Rate factor	1.216	3.356

Utilization ($0 copay)	400 days per year per 1,000 members
Average daily fee-for-service charge	$1,200

Skilled nursing facility care	25.2 days per year per 1,000 members
Current average daily cost	$430
Inpatient mental care ($0 copay)	64.4 days per year per 1,000 members
Current average daily cost	$540
Hospital-based surgery ($0 copay)	41.7 cases per year per 1,000 members
Current costs	$1,300 per case
Emergency room care ($15 copay)	132 visits per year per 1,000 members
Current costs	$190 per visit (see note)

Note: The emergency room cost of $190 is the total charge for facility services, some of which would be covered by the $15 copayment.

TABLE 5.5
Consortium Employee
Utilization and Cost Data:
Other Facility Services

Current number of visits ($5 copay)	3.4 per year per member

Note: New England routinely pays primary care physicians a capitated amount based on annual compensation of $175,000. New England assumes that one primary care physician can handle 4,000 patient visits per year.

TABLE 5.6
Consortium Employee
Utilization and Cost Data:
Primary Care Services

Current number of visits ($0 copay)	1.1 per year per member
Current cost per visit	$56.42

TABLE 5.7
Consortium Employee
Utilization and Cost Data:
Specialist Office Visits

Also, note that the premium calculation in Table 5.1 does not include certain medical services such as routine vision and dental care, chiropractic services, durable medical equipment, out-of-network services, and pharmacy benefits. The consortium specifically requested that the initial premium bid exclude such "rider" services. However, if New England is chosen to submit a final premium bid, the consortium will likely request pricing on one or more riders.

Finally, with no guidance from the consortium regarding the level of services desired or the copay structure, New England intends to offer three choices to the consortium: low cost, moderate cost, and high cost. Of course, these plans differ in that the low-cost (to the consortium) plan requires higher copays by employees and has more limitations on covered services; the high-cost plan has lower copays and fewer limitations; and the moderate-cost plan falls between the two extremes.

Assume that you have recently joined New England HMO as a marketing analyst. Your first task is to develop the bid presentation to be made to the consortium.

SUN CITY COMMUNITY HOSPITAL

6

BREAKEVEN ANALYSIS

SUN CITY COMMUNITY HOSPITAL (SCCH), an acute care hospital with 300 beds and 160 staff physicians, is one of 75 hospitals owned and operated by Health Services of America, a for-profit, publicly owned company. Although there are two other acute care hospitals serving the same general population, SCCH historically has been highly profitable because of its well-appointed facilities, fine medical staff, reputation for quality care, and the amount of individual attention it gives to its patients. In addition to inpatient services, SCCH operates an emergency room within the hospital complex and a stand-alone walk-in clinic located across the street from the area's major shopping mall, about two miles from the hospital.

In spite of its overall financial soundness, Mike Reynolds, SCCH's CEO, is concerned about the hospital's walk-in clinic. About ten years ago, all three area hospitals jumped onto the walk-in clinic bandwagon, and within a short time, there were five clinics scattered around the city. Now, only three are left, and none of them appears to be a big money maker. Mike wonders if SCCH should continue to operate its clinic or close it down. The clinic is currently handling a patient load of 45 visits per day, but it has the physical capacity to handle many more visits— up to 85 a day. Mike's decision has been complicated by the fact that Rose Daniels, SCCH's marketing director, has been pushing to embark on a new marketing program for the clinic. She believes that an expanded marketing effort aimed at local businesses would bring in the number of new patients needed to make the clinic a financial success.

Mike has asked Brent Williams, SCCH's CFO, to look into the whole matter of the walk-in clinic. In their meeting, Mike stated that he visualizes three potential outcomes for the clinic: (1) the clinic could be closed; (2) the clinic could continue to operate as is—that is, without expanding its marketing program; or (3) the clinic could continue to operate, but with the expanded marketing effort. As a starting point for the analysis, Brent has collected the most recent historical financial and operating data for the clinic, which are summarized in Table 6.1. In assessing the historical data, Brent noted that one competing clinic had recently (December 2002) closed its doors. Furthermore, a review of several years of financial data revealed that the SCCH clinic does not have a pronounced seasonal utilization pattern.

Next, Brent met several times with the clinic's director. The primary purpose of the meetings was to estimate the additional costs that would have to be borne if clinic usage rose above the current January/February average level of 45 visits per day. Any incremental usage would require additional expenditures for administrative and medical supplies, estimated to be $5.00 per patient visit for medical supplies, such as tongue blades and rubber gloves, and $2.00 per patient visit for administrative supplies, such as file folders and clinical record sheets.

Because of the relatively low utilization level, the clinic has purposely been staffed at the bare minimum. In fact, some clinic employees have started to grumble about not being able to do their jobs well because of overwork. Thus, any increase in the number of patient visits would require immediate administrative and medical staff increases. In addition, at an increase of 11 visits, the clinic would have to replace a part-time receptionist/record keeper with a full-time employee. At an additional 21 visits per day, another part-time nurse and physician would have to be added to the clinic's staff, and another part-time clerk would have to be hired if patient visits increased by 31 per day. The incremental costs associated with increased utilization are summarized in Table 6.2.

Brent also learned that the building is leased on a long-term basis. SCCH could cancel the lease, but the lease contract calls for a cancellation penalty of three months rent, or $37,500, at the current lease rate. In addition, Brent was startled to read in the newspaper that Baptist Hospital, SCCH's major competitor, had just bought the city's largest primary care group practice, and Baptist's CEO was quoted as saying that more group practice acquisitions are planned. Brent wondered

TABLE 6.1
SCCH Walk-In
Clinic: Historical
Financial Data

	CY 2002	Jan 2003	Feb 2003	Monthly Averages		
				2002	Jan/Feb 03	Total
Number of visits	14,522	1,365	1,335	1,210	1,350	1,230
Gross revenue	$578,237	$58,231	$57,996	$48,186	$58,114	$49,605
Allowance percentage	5.1%	5.5%	5.6%	5.1%	5.6%	5.2%
Net revenue	$548,747	$55,028	$54,748	$45,729	$54,888	$47,037
Salaries and wages	$154,250	$13,540	$13,544	$12,854	$13,542	$12,952
Physician fees	192,000	18,000	18,000	16,000	18,000	16,286
Malpractice insurance	31,440	3,215	3,215	2,620	3,215	2,705
Travel and education	5,365	538	665	447	602	469
General insurance	8,112	843	843	676	843	700
Subscriptions	189	0	0	16	0	14
Electricity	11,820	1,124	1,029	985	1,077	998
Water	1,260	135	142	105	139	110
Equipment rental	1,260	105	105	105	105	105
Building lease	155,745	12,500	12,500	12,979	12,500	12,910
Other operating expenses	103,779	8,152	7,923	8,648	8,038	8,561
Total operating expenses	$665,220	$58,152	$57,966	$55,435	$58,061	$55,810
Net profit (loss)	($116,473)	($3,124)	($3,218)	($9,706)	($3,173)	($8,773)
Gross margin (%)	-21.2%	-5.7%	-5.9%	-21.2%	-5.8%	-18.7%

TABLE 6.2
SCCH Walk-In
Clinic: Monthly
Incremental
Cost Data

	Number of Additional Visits per Day				
	0	*1–10*	*11–20*	*21–30*	*31–40*
Variable Costs					
Medical supplies			$5.00 per visit		
Administrative supplies			2.00 per visit		
Total variable costs per visit			$7.00 per visit		
Semifixed Costs					
Salaries and wages		$ 2,000	$ 3,000	$ 4,000	$ 5,000
Physician fees		8,000	8,000	16,000	16,000
Total monthly semifixed costs	$ 0	$10,000	$11,000	$20,000	$21,000
Fixed Costs					
Marketing assistant's salary	$ 3,000	$ 3,000	$ 3,000	$ 3,000	$ 3,000
Advertising expenses	2,000	2,000	2,000	2,000	2,000
Total monthly fixed costs	$ 5,000	$ 5,000	$ 5,000	$ 5,000	$ 5,000

whether Baptist's actions would influence the decision regarding the clinic's fate.

Finally, Brent met with SCCH's marketing director (Rose Daniels) to learn more about the proposed expansion of the clinic's marketing program. The primary focus of the new marketing program would be on occupational health services (OHS). OHS involves providing medical care to local businesses, including physical examinations for managers and employees; treatment of illnesses that occur during working hours; and treatment of work-related injuries, especially those covered by workers' compensation. Although some of the clinic's current business is OHS-related, Rose believes that a strong marketing effort, coupled with specialized OHS record keeping, could bring additional patients to the clinic. The proposed marketing expansion requires a marketing assistant who will run the clinic's OHS program. Additionally, the new marketing program would incur advertising costs for newspaper, radio, and TV ads as well as for brochures and handouts. The incremental costs associated with the new marketing program are also summarized in Table 6.2.

With a blank spreadsheet on the screen, Brent began to construct a model that would provide the information needed to help the board make a rational, informed decision. At first, Brent planned to conduct a standard capital budgeting analysis that focused on the profitability of the clinic as measured by net present value (NPV) or internal rate of return (IRR). Then, he realized that the expanded marketing program requires no capital investment. He also realized that no valid data are available on the incremental increase in visits that would be generated either by an increasing population base or by the expanded marketing program. Finally, he remembered that Mike requested that the analysis consider the inherent profitability of the clinic without the expanded marketing program.

With these points in mind, Brent thought that a breakeven analysis would be very useful in making the final decision. Specifically, he wanted to develop answers to the following questions:

1. What is the projected profitability of the walk-in clinic for the entire year if utilization continues at its current level?
2. How many additional visits per day would be required to break even without the new marketing program?
3. How many additional visits per day would be required to break even assuming that the new marketing program is undertaken?
4. How many additional daily visits would the new program have to bring in to make it worthwhile, regardless of the overall profitability of the clinic?

Finally, in earlier conversations, Mike also wondered if the clinic could "inflate" its way to profitability; that is, if utilization remained at its current level, could the clinic be expected to become profitable in, say, five years, solely because of inflationary increases in revenues? Overall, Brent must consider all relevant factors—both quantitative and qualitative—and come up with a reasonable recommendation regarding the future of the clinic.

VENTURE
MENTAL
HEALTH

VARIANCE ANALYSIS

7

VENTURE MENTAL HEALTH is a not-for-profit, multidisciplinary mental health provider that offers both inpatient and outpatient services on a full-risk (capitated) basis to members of managed care plans. Its clinical staff consists primarily of psychiatrists, psychologists, psychiatric nurses, social workers, and chemical dependency counselors. Currently, Venture has major contracts with two large managed care organizations in its service area: Physician Care (PC) and Share Healthplans (SH). Each of these organizations has both commercial and Medicare HMO contracts with Venture. Thus, in total, there are four separate product lines.

Venture is partially funded by state and local governments. The agreement with the funding agencies is that funds received would be used to cover overhead and capital expenses. Furthermore, expenses for drugs and other medical and administrative supplies are billed separately to the HMOs at cost. Thus, overhead and supplies expenses are not part of this budget, which means that the analysis focuses on clinical labor expenses. If the assumption is made that other payment mechanisms cover overhead, capital expenses, and supplies at cost, then Venture's profitability is solely a function of its ability to create revenues that exceed labor costs. Thus, its operating budget focuses on enrollment, per member premiums, utilization, and labor costs.

Table 7.1 contains the assumptions used to prepare Venture's 2002 operating budget. Note that the four product lines are expected to provide a total of 4,551,000 member-months of revenue during 2002. Also,

TABLE 7.1
Venture Mental Health:
2002 Operating Budget
Assumptions

Expected Enrollment (Member-Months)

PC Commercial	3,365,000
PC Medicare	469,000
SH Commercial	502,000
SH Medicare	215,000
Total	4,551,000

Expected Premium Data (per Member per Month)

PC Commercial	$0.65
PC Medicare	0.81
SH Commercial	0.58
SH Medicare	0.72

Expected Labor Data per Admission or Session

	Inpatient		Outpatient	
	# of Hours	Hourly Rate	# of Hours	Hourly Rate
PC Commercial	53.74	$35	1.04	$100
PC Medicare	68.43	35	1.30	100
SH Commercial	47.77	35	1.15	100
SH Medicare	56.86	35	1.14	100

note that each product line has a different PMPM payment (premium) amount. Table 7.1 also contains expected admission (for inpatients), referral rate (for outpatients), and labor cost and utilization data for each product line. Because of the unique employment arrangements between Venture and its clinical staff, in which they are paid on the basis of the number of patient service units provided, clinical labor costs are virtually all variable, and hence costs are not identified as fixed or variable.

Table 7.2 contains the forecasted 2002 budget. In essence, data from Table 7.1 are used to forecast revenues and costs, both in the aggregate and by product line. Overall, Venture expected to earn a profit of $129,828 on these product lines in 2002.

Expected Utilization and Total Labor Cost Data

Plan Type	Avg # Members (in 000s)	Inpatient			Outpatient			Total
		Admission Rate	Cost per Admission	Total Costs	Referral Rate	Cost per Session	Total Costs	
PC:								
Commercial	280.417	3.81	$1,881	$2,009,639	2.00	$104	$58,327	$2,067,966
Medicare	39.083	3.96	2,395	370,671	2.00	130	10,162	380,833
Total	319.500			$2,380,310			$68,489	$2,448,799
SH:								
Commercial	41.833	3.89	$1,672	$272,085	2.00	$115	$9,622	$281,707
Medicare	17.917	4.17	1,990	148,681	2.00	114	4,085	152,766
Total	59.750			$420,766			$13,707	$434,473
Grand total	379.250			$2,801,076			$82,196	$2,883,272

TABLE 7.1
(continued)
Venture Mental Health:
2002 Operating Budget
Assumptions

TABLE 7.2
Venture Mental Health:
2002 Operating Budget

Expected Aggregate Profit

Revenues

PC Commercial	3,365,000 x $0.65 =	$2,187,250
PC Medicare	469,000 x $0.81 =	379,890
SH Commercial	502,000 x $0.58 =	291,160
SH Medicare	215,000 x $0.72 =	154,800
Total		$3,013,100

Costs (from Table 7.1)

PC Commercial	$2,067,966
PC Medicare	380,833
SH Commercial	281,707
SH Medicare	152,766
Total	$2,883,272
Profit	$ 129,828
Margin	4.3%

Expected Product Line Profits

	PC		SH		
	Commercial	Medicare	Commercial	Medicare	Total
Revenue	$2,187,250	$ 379,890	$ 291,160	$ 154,800	$3,013,100
Costs	2,067,966	380,833	281,707	152,766	2,883,272
Profit	$ 119,284	($ 943)	$ 9,453	$ 2,034	$ 129,828
Margin	5.4%	(0.2%)	3.2%	1.3%	4.3%

During the first quarter of 2002, Venture's managers noted a higher utilization rate than budgeted. To add to their concern, the monthly enrollment figures supplied by the contracting managed care plans were less than those budgeted. Together, these trends indicated lower revenues and higher per enrollee costs, and hence lower profits, than forecasted in Table 7.2, although a higher premium amount on one plan partially offset the lower enrollment. These concerns were borne out when the first quarter profits came in under budget. To help stem the adverse trend, Venture's managers instituted a utilization management system in which all inpatient stays were required to be approved by the clinic's medical director—a senior staff psychiatrist.

Unfortunately, the action taken was "too little, too late" to save the year. Table 7.3 contains operating results for 2002, while Table 7.4 contains the realized aggregate and product line P&L statements. A quick review of Table 7.4 reveals that the signals conveyed by the first quarter data were indeed correct—2002 ended with a loss.

When the results were submitted to Venture's CEO, Janet Johnson, she grimaced and said, "I knew it was coming, but I did not expect the year to be that bad." It was immediately apparent to Janet that Venture could not afford similar results in 2003. She knew that something had to be done, but the best course of action was not clear.

TABLE 7.3
Venture Mental Health: 2002 Operating Results

Actual Enrollment (Member-Months)

PC Commercial	3,073,133
PC Medicare	485,000
SH Commercial	547,105
SH Medicare	257,000
Total	4,362,238

Actual Premium Data (per Member per Month)

PC Commercial	$0.60
PC Medicare	0.81
SH Commercial	0.58
SH Medicare	0.72

Actual Labor Data per Admission or Session

	Inpatient		Outpatient	
	# of Hours	Hourly Rate	# of Hours	Hourly Rate
PC Commercial	47.32	$38	0.95	$109.50
PC Medicare	58.66	38	1.15	109.50
SH Commercial	52.06	33	0.98	95
SH Medicare	84.85	33	2.00	95

**TABLE 7.3
(continued)
Venture Mental Health:
2002 Operating Results**

Actual Utilization and Cost Data

Plan Type	Avg # Members (in 000s)	Inpatient			Outpatient			Total
		Admission Rate	Cost per Admission	Total Costs	Referral Rate	Cost per Session	Total Costs	
PC:								
Commercial	256.094	4.33	$1,798	$1,993,782	3.65	$104	$ 97,213	$2,090,996
Medicare	40.417	4.68	2,229	421,615	1.86	126	9,472	431,087
Total	296.511			$2,415,397			$106,685	$2,522,083
SH:								
Commercial	45.592	5.79	$1,718	$ 453,514	3.35	$ 93	$ 14,204	$ 467,719
Medicare	21.417	4.56	2,800	273,448	1.75	190	7,121	280,569
Total	67.009			$ 726,962			$ 21,325	$ 748,288
Grand total	363.520			$3,142,360			$128,011	$3,270,371

Note: These data were generated on a spreadsheet, and hence some rounding differences occur.

TABLE 7.4
Venture Mental Health:
2002 Actual P&L
Statements

Aggregate Profit Results

Revenues

PC Commercial	3,073,113 x $0.60 =	$1,843,880
PC Medicare	485,000 x $0.81 =	392,850
SH Commercial	547,105 x $0.58 =	317,321
SH Medicare	257,000 x $0.72 =	185,040
Total		$2,739,091

Costs (from Table 7.3)

PC Commercial	$2,090,996
PC Medicare	431,087
SH Commercial	467,719
SH Medicare	280,569
Total	$3,270,371
Profit	($ 531,280)
Margin	(19.4%)

Product Line Profit Results

	PC		SH		
	Commercial	Medicare	Commercial	Medicare	Total
Revenue	$1,843,880	$392,850	$317,321	$185,040	$2,739,091
Costs	2,090,996	431,087	467,719	280,569	3,270,371
Profit	($ 247,116)	($ 38,237)	($150,398)	($ 95,529)	($ 531,280)
Margin	(13.4%)	(9.7%)	(47.4%)	(51.6%)	(19.4%)

Note: These data were generated on a spreadsheet, and hence some rounding differences occur.

To help plan for next year, Janet asked Venture's finance and accounting department head, Bob Mitchell, to perform a variance analysis on the data to help identify the problems that led to the poor financial results for 2002. Unfortunately, Bob's area of expertise is dealing with lenders and other capital suppliers, so he passed the assignment on to you, a newly hired financial analyst.

FIGURE 7.1
Variance Analysis
Summary

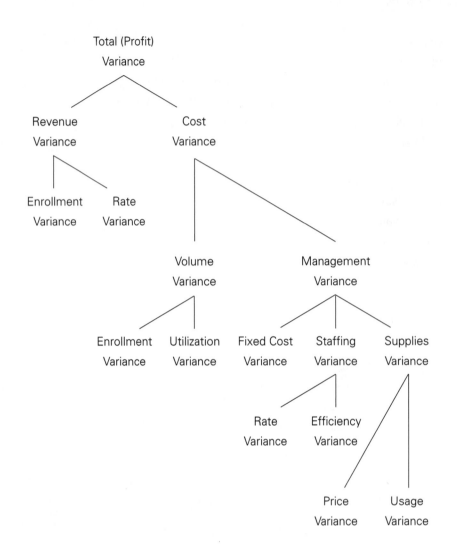

Hint: It might be useful to use this figure as the format for presenting your numerical results.

To start the analysis, you created a diagram (Figure 7.1) to help understand variance analysis. (Note that this diagram is generic in nature and has not been "customized" for this case.) Furthermore, you recognize that because the volume variance consists of differences in both enrollment and utilization, it is necessary to create two flexible budgets: one flexed (adjusted) for actual enrollment only, and a second one

		TABLE 7.5 **Generic** **Equation List**
Total variance	= Actual profit – Static profit.	
Revenue variance	= Actual revenue – Static revenue.	
Enrollment variance	= Flexible (enrollment) revenue – Static revenue.	
Rate variance	= Actual revenue – Flexible (enrollment) revenue.	
Cost variance	= Static costs – Actual costs.	
Volume variance	= Flexible (enrollment/utilization) profit – Static profit.	
Enrollment variance	= Flexible (enrollment) profit – Static profit.	
Utilization variance	= Flexible (enrollment/utilization) profit – Flexible (enrollment) profit.	
Management variance	= Actual profit – Flexible (enrollment/utilization) profit.	
Fixed cost variance	= Flexible fixed costs – Actual fixed costs.	
Staffing variance	= Flexible (enrollment/utilization) staffing costs – Actual staffing costs.	
Rate variance	= (Static hourly labor rate – Actual hourly labor rate) x Actual number of hours per episode x Actual utilization rate x Actual enrollment.	
Efficiency variance	= (Expected number of hours per episode – Actual number of hours per episode) x Expected hourly labor rate x Actual utilization rate x Actual enrollment.	
Supplies variance	= Flexible (enrollment/utilization) supplies costs – Actual supplies costs.	
Price variance	= (Static price – Actual price) x Actual units.	
Usage variance	= (Flexible units – Actual units) x Static price.	

Note: Not all of the above equations are necessarily useful to all product lines. Also, some definitions, when applied to costs, may be reversed to make a negative variance value indicate an unfavorable outcome.

flexed for both actual enrollment and actual utilization. Additionally, to help with the calculations, you jotted down an equation list for calculating variances. (Note that not all of the equations listed are necessarily applicable to this analysis.) This list is contained in Table 7.5.

Of course, both Janet and Bob are more concerned with what the numbers mean than what the numbers are. Therefore, your variance analysis should include a great deal of interpretation along with the numbers. Finally, you would like to use this assignment to help advance your career within the organization, so you are going to go one step further. You plan to offer recommendations for management action along with the numbers and interpretation.

BEAVER CREEK CLINIC

CASH BUDGETING

8

BEAVER CREEK is an upscale winter resort located a short distance from Vail, Colorado. Beaver Creek Clinic is a small walk-in clinic located adjacent to the primary ski area that specializes in the treatment of injuries sustained while skiing. It is owned and operated by two physicians: James Peterson, an orthopedist, and Amanda Cook, an internist. The clinic has an outside accountant who takes care of payroll matters, but Dr. Cook does all the other financial work for the clinic. However, to help in that task, the clinic recently hired a part-time MBA student, Doug Washington.

On a Wednesday afternoon in October 2002, Dr. Cook called Doug into her office to tell him that she had just received a phone call from the head of commercial lending at First Bank of Denver, the clinic's primary lender. Because of a forecasted reduction in bank deposits, and hence funds available to make commercial loans, First Bank has asked each of its commercial loan customers for an estimate of its borrowing requirements for the first half of 2003.

Dr. Cook had a previously scheduled meeting at First Bank the following Monday to discuss cash management services, so she asked Doug to come up with an estimate of the clinic's line of credit requirements to submit at the meeting. A line of credit is a short-term loan agreement by which a bank agrees to lend a business some specified maximum amount. The business can borrow ("draw down") against the credit line at any time it is in force, which is usually no longer than one year. When a line expires, it will have to be renegotiated if it is still

TABLE 8.1
Beaver Creek Clinic:
Billings Forecast

Year	Month	Amount
2002	November	$150,000
	December	250,000
2003	January	350,000
	February	450,000
	March	300,000
	April	150,000
	May	100,000
	June	175,000
	July	250,000
	August	200,000

needed. The amount borrowed on the line, or some lesser amount, can be repaid at any time, but the full amount borrowed must be repaid at expiration. Typically, interest is charged daily on the amount drawn down, and a commitment fee is required upfront to secure the line. In general, lines of credit are used by businesses to meet temporary (usually seasonal) cash needs, as opposed to being used for permanent financing.

Dr. Cook was going on vacation, a trip that had already been delayed several times, and she would not be back until just before her meeting at the bank. Therefore, she asked Doug to prepare a cash budget while she was away. No one had taken the time to prepare a cash budget recently, although a spreadsheet model that had been constructed a few years ago was available for use. From information previously developed, Doug knew that no seasonal financing would be needed from First Bank before January, so he decided to restrict his budget to the period from January through June 2003. As a first step, he looked through the clinic's financial records to get the data needed to develop the billings forecast contained in Table 8.1.

Patient volume at the clinic is highly seasonal because the vast majority of the business occurs during the ski season, which generally runs from December through March. In fact, at one time Drs. Peterson and Cook thought about closing the clinic during the slow months, but (1) it would be very difficult to operate efficiently for only a portion of the year and (2) the area has started to attract a sizable amount of summer visitors, which has made summer operations more financially attractive.

Again, on the basis of previous experience, Doug was able to convert billings for medical services into actual cash collections. On average, about 20 percent of the clinic's patients pay immediately for services rendered. Third-party payers pay the remaining claims, with 20 percent of the payments made within 30 days and the 60 percent remainder paid within 60 days. For monthly budgeting purposes, patient payments (20 percent) are assumed to be collected in the month of billing, 20 percent are assumed to be collected in the month following the billing month, and 60 percent are assumed to be collected two months after the month of billing.

Variable medical costs at the clinic are assumed to consist entirely of medical and administrative supplies. These supplies, which are estimated to cost 15 percent of billings, are purchased two months before expected usage. On average, the clinic pays about half of its suppliers in the month of purchase (two months before use) and the other half in the following month (one month before use).

Clinical labor costs (for physicians and nurses) are the primary expense of the clinic. During the high season (December through March), these costs run $150,000 a month, but some of the nursing staff work only seasonally, so clinical labor costs drop to $120,000 a month in the remaining months.

The clinic pays fixed general and administrative expenses, including clerical labor, of approximately $30,000 a month, while lease obligations amount to $12,000 per month. These expenditures are expected to continue at the same level throughout the forecast period. The clinic's miscellaneous expenses are estimated to be $10,000 monthly.

The clinic has a semi-annual, five-year, 10 percent, $500,000 term loan outstanding with First Bank that has amortization payments of $64,752, which are due on March 15 and September 15. Also, the clinic is planning to replace an old x-ray machine (which has no salvage value) in February with a new one costing $125,000. The clinic is a partnership, so, for tax purposes, any profits (or losses) are pro-rated to the two physician partners, who must pay individual taxes on this income. Thus, no tax payments are built into the cash budget.

The clinic has to maintain a minimum cash balance of $50,000 at First Bank because of compensating balance requirements on its term loan. This amount, but no more, is expected to be on hand on January 1, 2003.

If a daily cash budget is required, some additional assumptions about volume and collections are required:

1. Beaver Creek Clinic operates seven days a week.
2. Patient volume is more or less constant throughout the month, so the daily billings forecast will be 1/(Number of days in the month) multiplied by the billings forecast for that month.
3. Daily billings follow the 20 percent, 20 percent, 60 percent collection breakdown based on monthly billings.
4. Patient payments are assumed to occur on the day of billing, "early" payers are assumed to pay 30 days after billing, and "late" payers are assumed to pay 60 days after billing.
5. The lease payment is made on the 1st of the month.
6. Fifty percent of both clinical labor costs and general and administrative expenses are paid on the 1st of the month, and 50 percent are paid on the 15th of the month.
7. Supplies are delivered on the 1st of the month and paid for on the 5th of the month.
8. Miscellaneous expenses are incurred and paid evenly throughout each month.
9. Term loan payments are made on the 15th of the month in which they are due.
10. The compensating balance of $50,000 must be in the bank on each day.

In addition to the cash budget itself, Dr. Cook asked Doug to consider several additional issues:

1. Will the clinic need to request a line of credit for the period and, if so, how big should the line be?
2. Perhaps a monthly budget may not reveal the full extent of the borrowing requirements actually needed. To see if her concern is valid, Dr. Cook suggested that

Doug construct a daily cash budget for the month of January as a test case.

3. The existing cash budget model does not provide for interest paid on line of credit borrowings or interest earned on cash surpluses. Dr. Cook suggested that the monthly cash budget be modified to include these items. Currently, the interest rate on First Bank line of credit draw downs is 8 percent compounded monthly (8%/12 = 0.667% per month), and First Bank pays 4 percent compounded monthly (4%/12 = 0.333% per month) on temporary investments of excess cash.

4. Although the target cash balance has been based on First Bank's compensating balance requirement, the term loan will be paid off in September 2003. Dr. Cook asked how the clinic might go about setting its target cash balance when no compensating balance is required.

5. Dr. Cook is well aware that the cash budget is a forecast, so most of the cash flows shown are expected values rather than amounts known with certainty. If actual patient billings, and hence collections, were different from forecasted levels, then the forecasted surpluses and deficits would be incorrect. Dr. Cook is very interested in knowing how various changes in key assumptions would affect the forecasted surplus or deficit. For example, if billings fell below the forecasted level or if collections were stretched out, what effect would that have?

6. Finally, Dr. Cook believes that the surge in patient volume over the forecast period is bound to result in some cash surpluses, and she wants to know what the clinic should do with them.

Place yourself in Doug's position. Be prepared to discuss your analysis with Dr. Cook when you meet with her next week.

CHRISTCHURCH TRANSPLANT CENTER

MARGINAL COST PRICING ANALYSIS

9

CHRISTCHURCH TRANSPLANT CENTER (the Center), which is part of the Princess Margaret Healthcare System (the System), is a regional leader in the very intense and medically sophisticated area of organ transplants. All transplants are performed at Christchurch General Hospital (the Hospital), the 400-bed flagship of the System.

Craig MacLeod, the director of the Center, has been with the System for ten years, during which time significant growth occurred in both the number of transplant programs and the volume of procedures performed. When Craig joined the System he was put in charge of a kidney transplant program that was averaging 60 transplants per year and a heart transplant program that was performing 40 transplants per year. Today, the Center performs over 300 transplants annually, including transplants from the newly initiated liver, lung, and pancreas programs.

As a teaching institution, the Hospital is affiliated with a local university. The Center's physicians are employed by the university, although their compensation is linked to some degree to the amount of clinical revenues that they generate. Still, the physicians tend to be underpaid in comparison to their private practice colleagues, which leads to higher-than-average turnover. Craig was made painfully aware of this fact when the surgical director of the liver transplant program, and his good friend, left the university for a higher salary and the opportunity for more leisure time. He was replaced by newly hired Dr. Markham Lee, a physician who has a national reputation as a skilled transplant surgeon.

The liver transplant program is the most successful of all organ programs in terms of volume and revenues. Last year, volume totaled 120 transplants, and this year Craig is optimistic that the liver program can do even better. However, he knows that increased volume is largely dependent on the number of organ donors and his success in negotiating a new managed care contract with the VASE Network, the largest transplant benefits company in the nation.

Contracting for transplant services is unique and complex because of the sophistication of the medical procedures involved. Transplant services consist of five phases: (1) patient evaluation, (2) patient care while awaiting surgery, (3) organ procurement, (4) surgery and the attendant inpatient stay, and (5) one year of follow-up visits. The costs involved in Phase 1 are relatively simple to estimate, but the remaining phases can be extremely variable in resource utilization, and hence costs, because of differences in patient acuity and surgical outcomes.

Historically, transplant reimbursement has been handled in a number of different ways. Initially, many providers bundled all five phases together and offered insurers a single, global rate. Although this method simplified the contracting process, the rate set was often chosen more on the basis of building market share than on covering costs. Indeed, many institutions could not even estimate with any confidence the true costs of providing transplant services.

Somewhat ironically, success in gaining market share usually increases the financial risk of the transplant program because higher volumes increase the likelihood of higher acuity patients. Furthermore, changes in the organ allocation system have promoted the acceptance of sicker patients into transplant programs. Although the total costs associated with all phases of a liver transplant average about $250,000, the amount can more than quadruple if the patient requires a re-transplant or if other complications occur. Because of this extreme variability in costs, outlier protection is a critical aspect of managed care negotiations if the reimbursement methodology is a fixed prospective rate such as a global rate.

Craig's first meeting with the new liver transplant surgical director was extremely positive. Dr. Lee shared Craig's enthusiasm to build the liver program into one of the largest in the country. Furthermore, Craig was very impressed with Dr. Lee's desire to be directly involved in contract negotiations and his concern over the financial implications of each contract.

In his second meeting with Dr. Lee, Craig discussed the specifics of the current contract negotiations with the VASE Network. Phases 1, 2, and 5 will be reimbursed at a set discount from charges. Furthermore, to reduce the amount of financial risk borne by the Center, Phase 3 (organ procurement) will be reimbursed on a cost basis. This makes sense because the cost of Phase 3 is almost completely uncontrollable by the Center. Thus, the primary focus of the negotiations, and the make-or-break part of the contract, is the reimbursement amount for Phase 4.

In general, Phase 4 costs are divided into two categories: hospital costs and physician costs. Physician costs have already been agreed on, so the primary matter at hand involves only hospital costs. To aid in the negotiations, Craig compiled the Phase 4 hospital costs of 12 recent liver transplant patients. These data are presented in Table 9.1.

When Dr. Lee read the numbers, he was amazed. A total average cost of $119,805 for 19 days average length of stay translates to a per diem average cost of over $6,000. He was sure that the VASE Network would not be willing to sign a contract for Phase 4 hospital costs that exceeded $100,000. Indeed, he hoped that Phase 4 hospital costs could be held to $90,000 or less to ensure that the contract negotiations were successful. Thus, Dr. Lee suggested that alternative strategies be examined to see if these costs could be reduced.

At first glance, it appeared to Craig that a large cost savings could be realized by merely reducing the average length of stay (LOS). For example, it appeared that Phase 4 hospital costs associated with a particular patient could be reduced by over $12,000 by merely reducing the LOS by two days. However, further analysis revealed the costs associated with Phase 4 are not a linear function of LOS. Internal studies at the Center indicated that the first day of Phase 4 is usually the most costly while the last day is usually the least costly. Indeed, roughly 70 percent of Phase 4 costs occur in the first 24 hours of hospitalization.

When it appeared that it would be difficult to lower Phase 4 hospital costs, Craig decided to pursue a different strategy. He believed that economies of scale are present in liver transplants, and hence the marginal cost of each transplant is lower than the average cost. Thus, Craig proposed that the Phase 4 hospital contract rate be based on marginal rather than total (full) costs.

Assume that you have been hired as a consultant to recommend a fixed amount (the base rate) that should be proposed in the contract

TABLE 9.1
Statements of Operations
(millions of dollars)

Patient	Age	LOS	Total Cost	Nursing Cost	Ancillary Cost	OR Cost	Lab Cost	Radiology Cost	Drug Costs	Other Costs
A	61	25	$141,092	$10,261	$65,416	$6,770	$13,712	$1,483	$20,992	$22,458
B	56	15	139,306	11,969	63,668	8,501	7,409	2,261	24,504	20,994
C	42	12	74,259	6,939	33,661	3,128	5,279	668	6,964	17,620
D	52	13	115,349	7,221	54,063	5,779	6,112	903	7,638	33,633
E	12	26	172,613	28,205	72,204	6,847	10,550	1,766	23,061	29,980
F	59	22	83,807	16,858	33,474	4,654	6,211	1,397	9,698	11,515
G	41	25	136,060	9,645	63,208	6,489	13,091	1,382	20,127	22,118
H	35	17	139,308	11,969	63,669	8,501	7,409	2,261	24,505	20,994
I	52	12	74,259	6,939	33,660	3,128	5,280	668	6,964	17,620
J	38	13	115,348	7,221	54,063	5,778	6,111	903	7,639	33,633
K	59	25	166,224	26,909	69,657	6,765	10,061	1,677	22,007	29,148
L	60	21	80,034	15,629	32,202	4,531	5,937	1,293	9,122	11,320
Average	47	19	$119,805	$13,314	$53,245	$5,906	$8,097	$1,389	$15,268	$22,586

negotiations for Phase 4 hospital services. To help in the analysis, Craig has indicated that approximately 60 percent of nursing, ancillary, operating room (OR), and laboratory costs are fixed. The remaining costs — laboratory, radiology, drug, and other services — are predominantly variable.

In addition, you have been asked to recommend a method for handling outliers, including the threshold amount and additional reimbursement scheme. Other programs within the Center use two methods for outlier payments. One method is to charge an additional per diem amount based on a LOS threshold. Alternatively, some percentage of costs above the base rate can be charged when a cost threshold is reached.

GOTHAM HEALTH NETWORK

10

ABC ANALYSIS

GOTHAM HEALTH NETWORK (the Network), which is a newly created subsidiary of Gotham Health System (the System), consists of five medical group practices. When initially acquired, the practices were placed in a for-profit subsidiary, but concerns over both Stark Law provisions and the fact that the practices were barely profitable prompted the System to move them to a new not-for-profit subsidiary.

The practices include both primary care and specialty physicians, with an emphasis on obstetrics/gynecology, surgery, pediatrics, and psychology. Although the physicians are administratively organized into five groups, they practice at only three different locations, each one staffed with a physician mix of primary care and specialists. In spite of the fact that it does not contribute directly to profitability, the Network is considered to be essential to the System because it generates a large amount of indirect income from both inpatient referrals and outpatient ancillary services. In fact, it has been estimated that each dollar of revenue generated by the Network leads to eight dollars of inpatient and ancillary revenues. By limiting the amount of ancillary services provided at the Network locations, patients are forced (or at least encouraged) to utilize Gotham Hospital (the Hospital), the founder of the System, for such services.

Still, some ancillary services are best performed at the Network locations for one or more of the following reasons: lower costs, increased physician efficiency, or improved patient convenience. For example, one of the practice locations now has its own diagnostic imaging capability. When it was moved from the Hospital to the Network, volume increased, costs decreased, and both physician and patient satisfaction improved.

The proposal now being considered by the Network is to provide ultrasound services at the Network locations. Preliminary analysis indicates that two approaches are most suitable. Alternative I involves the purchase of one ultrasound machine for each of the Network's three locations. Patients would schedule appointments, generally at the clinic that they are using, during pre-set times on particular days of the week. Then, the full-time ultrasound technician would travel from one location to another to administer the tests as scheduled. In Alternative II, patient scheduling would be the same, but only one ultrasound machine would be purchased. It would be mounted in a van that the technician would drive to each of the three Network locations. Most of the operating costs are identical between the two alternatives, but Alternative II has the added cost of operating the van and setting up the machine after each move.

The two alternatives differ substantially in capital costs because Alternative I requires three ultrasound machines, at a cost of $75,000 each, while Alternative II requires only one. However, Alternative II requires a van, which with necessary modifications would cost $40,000. Thus, the capital costs for Alternative I total 3 x $75,000 = $225,000, while those for Alternative II amount to only $75,000 + $40,000 = $115,000.

Note, though, that because the two alternatives have different operating costs, a proper cost analysis of the two alternatives must include both capital and operating costs. The Network financial staff, which in reality is the System financial staff, considered several methods for estimating the operating costs of each alternative. After much discussion, the CFO decided that the activity based costing (ABC) method would be best. Furthermore, an ad hoc taskforce was assigned the task of performing the cost analysis.

To begin the ABC analysis, the taskforce had to develop the activities involved in the two alternatives. This was accomplished by conducting "walk-throughs" of the entire process from the standpoints of the patient, the ultrasound technician, and the billing and collections department. The results are contained in Table 10.1. A review of the activities confirms that all except one—transportation and setup—are applicable to both alternatives.

1. Schedule the appointment
2. Patient check-in
3. Ultrasound testing
4. Patient check-out
5. Film processing
6. Film reading
7. Billing and collection
8. General administration
9. Transportation and setup (Alternative II only)

TABLE 10.1
Activities Associated with Alternatives I and II

The next step in the ABC process is to detail the costs associated with each activity. This step uses financial, operational, and volume data, along with the appropriate cost driver for each activity, to estimate resource consumption. Note that traditional costing, which often focuses on department-level costs, typically first deals with direct costs and then allocates indirect (overhead) costs proportionally according to a predetermined allocation rate. In ABC costing, the activities required to produce some service, including both direct and indirect, are estimated simultaneously. For example, Table 10.1 contains activities that entail direct costs (such as technician time) and activities that entail indirect costs (such as billing and collections). Although the ABC method is more complex, and hence costlier, than the traditional method, it is the only way to accurately (more or less) estimate the costs of individual procedures.

Activity cost detail on a per procedure basis is contained in Table 10.2. In essence, each activity is assigned a cost driver that is most highly correlated with the actual utilization of resources. Then the number of driver units, along with the cost per unit, is estimated for each activity. The product of the number of units and the cost per unit gives the cost of each activity. Finally, the activity costs are summed to obtain the total per procedure cost.

Many of the activity costs cannot be estimated without an estimate of the number of ultrasounds that will be performed. The best estimate is that 50 procedures would be done each week, regardless of which alternative is chosen. Assuming the technician works 48 weeks per year, the annual volume estimate is 2,400 procedures. Of course, one of the factors that complicates the analysis is that a much greater total volume

TABLE 10.2
Activity Cost Detail

Activity	Cost Driver	Volume	Cost per Unit
Schedule the appointment	Receptionist time	3 minutes	$ 0.20
Patient check-in	Receptionist time	5 minutes	0.20
Ultrasound testing	Technician time	45 minutes	0.40
	Physician time	1.5 minutes	3.00
	Supplies	per procedure	9.00
Patient check-out	Receptionist time	5 minutes	0.20
Film processing	Technician time	10 minutes	0.40
Film reading	Contract terms	per procedure	40.00
Billing and collection	Overhead costs	per procedure	6.80
General administration	Overhead costs	per procedure	1.25
Transportation and setup	Technician time	6 minutes	1.00

Notes:
1. Physician time for testing (15 minutes) is needed for one of every 10 patients.
2. Supplies consist of linen, probe cover, gel, film, and print paper.
3. There are no radiologists in the Network. Films will be read by the Hospital's radiologists at a contract fee of $40 per procedure.
4. Billing and collection costs are based on an average cost per medical services bill.
5. General administration costs are based on an estimate of facilities and other administrative costs.
6. Transportation and setup is based on ten procedures per day at each location and includes vehicle operating costs.

can be accommodated under Alternative I, with three machines, than with Alternative II, with only one machine. However, to keep the initial analysis manageable, the decision was made to assume the same annual volume regardless of the alternative chosen.

Finally, to have a rough estimate of total annual costs over the life of the equipment, it is necessary to make assumptions about the useful life of the ultrasound machines and the van. Although somewhat controversial, the decision was made to assume a five-year life for both the ultrasound machines and the van. Furthermore, the assumption was made that the value of these assets would be negligible at the end of five years.

Assume that you are the chairperson of the ad hoc taskforce. Your charge is to evaluate the two alternatives and to make a recommendation on which one to accept, assuming that revenues would be identical for the two alternatives, and hence the decision can be made solely on the basis of costs. As part of the analysis, it will be necessary to estimate the costs of the two alternatives on a per procedure and annual basis. In addition, any qualitative factors that are relevant to the decision must be considered before the recommendation is made.

To keep the analysis manageable, the taskforce was instructed to assume that operating costs remain constant over the useful life of the equipment. For comparative purposes, this assumption is not too egregious because the activities are roughly the same for both alternatives, and hence inflation would have a somewhat neutral impact on costs.

In addition to the base case analysis, the System CFO has asked the taskforce to perform some sensitivity (scenario) analyses. First, he is concerned about the accuracy of the cost detail inputs. Although there is some confidence in many of the estimates, others are more arbitrary. Those activity cost inputs that are considered to be most uncertain are supplies cost per unit, billing and collection cost per unit, general administration cost per unit, and transportation and setup cost per unit. Thus, the taskforce has been asked to redo the analysis assuming that these inputs are higher than the base case values by 10 and 20 percent. Activity cost inputs less than the base case values could also be examined, but the critical issue here is not to underestimate the total costs involved in the two alternatives.

Along the same lines, the taskforce was also asked what would happen to the cost estimates if the useful life of the capital equipment was as short as three years or as long as seven years. Also, there was some concern expressed that the useful life of the equipment depended on the alternative chosen; that is, there would be less wear and tear under Alternative I than under Alternative II.

Although you believe that it also would be very useful to perform a sensitivity analysis on the number of procedures, this task would require recalculation of the per unit cost inputs, an effort thought to be too time consuming to undertake at this point in the analysis.

Financial Management Basics

PUGET SOUND SURGERY CENTERS

TIME VALUE ANALYSIS

11

GARY HUDSON was born and raised in Tacoma, Washington. He obtained his bachelor's degree in business from Oregon State University, where he enrolled in the NROTC program, and, after graduation, he received a commission in the U.S. Marine Corps. After his release from active duty, Gary used his GI Bill benefits to obtain a master's degree in health services administration. His first job in healthcare was as a special projects coordinator/financial analyst at a large Portland hospital. He enjoyed his work there, but his ultimate goal was to return to Tacoma as the manager of a smaller healthcare business, where he would have more responsibility and authority. After five years in Portland, Gary became the chief operating officer of Puget Sound Surgery Centers, an investor-owned chain of ambulatory surgery centers with six locations in the Seattle/Tacoma area.

Immediately after assuming his new position, Gary faced several decisions. First, the company currently has $100,000 in its cash account, but its target cash balance is only $50,000. Thus, Gary wants to temporarily invest the excess $50,000 in marketable securities, which typically consist of low-risk, short-term securities such as Treasury bills or money market mutual funds. One alternative that Gary is considering is to invest the $50,000 in a bank certificate of deposit (CD). CDs are generally available in maturities from six months to ten years, and interest can be handled in one of two ways: the investor (buyer) can receive periodic interest payments or the interest can automatically be reinvested in the CD. In the latter case, the buyer receives no interest during the life of the CD but receives the accumulated interest plus principal amount at maturity. Because the goal of this investment is to accumulate funds for future use, as opposed to generate current income, all interest earned on the CD would be reinvested.

Second, the company recently bought a new hardware/software system to handle its patient billings. However, it is obvious, even now, that the current system will have to be replaced with an even more sophisticated system in about five years. After making some inquiries to potential vendors, Gary estimates the future cost of the new system to be $200,000. To ensure that the funds are available to make this purchase, Gary is planning either to deposit a lump sum today in an interest-bearing account or to make annual payments into the same account.

Third, Puget Sound Surgery Centers has some extra space at one of its locations that it might lease out for five years. The initial renovation cost, which includes new flooring and lighting as well as a new outside entrance, is estimated to be $40,000. Because of some unusual terms in the proposed lease contract, and also because of a promise to add additional computer ports in three years, the net cash inflows expected from the lease follow this uneven pattern:

End of Year	Net Cash Flow
1	$ 12,000
2	14,000
3	2,000
4	16,000
5	20,000

The decisions that Gary faces all involve time value analysis. As a check on your skills, see if you can answer the following relevant questions:

1. Consider the $50,000 excess cash. Assume that Gary invests the funds in a one-year CD.
   a. What is the CD's value at maturity (future value) if it pays 10.0 percent (annual) interest?
   b. What would be its future value if the CD pays 5.0 percent interest? If it pays 15.0 percent interest?

c. BankWest offers CDs with 10.0 percent nominal (stated) interest, but compounded semiannually. What is the effective annual rate on this CD? What would the future value be after one year if $50,000 were invested?

d. The Tacoma Branch of Bank of America offers a 10.0 percent CD with daily compounding. What is the CD's effective annual rate and its value at maturity one year from now if $50,000 is invested? (Assume a 365-day year.)

e. What stated rate would BankWest have to offer to make its semiannual-compounding CD competitive with Bank of America's daily-compounding CD?

2. Rework Parts (a) through (d) of Question 1 assuming that each CD has a five-year maturity.

3. Now consider the surgery centers' goal of having $200,000 available in five years to buy a new patient billing system.

a. What lump sum amount must be invested today in a CD paying 10.0 percent annual interest to accumulate the needed $200,000?

b. What annual interest rate is needed to produce $200,000 after five years if only $100,000 is invested?

4. Now consider a second alternative for accumulating funds to buy the new billing system. In lieu of a lump sum investment, assume that five annual payments of $32,000 are made at the end of each year.

a. What type of annuity is this?

b. What is the present value of this annuity if the opportunity cost rate is 10.0 percent annually? 10.0 percent compounded semiannually?

c. What is the future value of this annuity if the payments are invested in an account paying 10.0 percent interest annually? 10.0 percent compounded semiannually?

    d. What annual interest rate is required to accumulate the $200,000 needed to make the purchase assuming a $32,000 annual payment?

    e. What size annual payment would be needed to accumulate $200,000 under annual compounding at a 10.0 percent interest rate?

    f. Suppose the payments are only $16,000 each, but they are made every six months, starting six months from now. What would be the future value if the ten payments were invested at 10.0 percent annual interest? If they were invested at BankWest at 10.0 percent, compounded semiannually?

5. Assume now that the payments are made at the beginning of each period. Repeat the analysis in Question 4.

6. Now consider the uneven cash flow stream stemming from the lease agreement given in the case.

    a. What is the present (Year 0) value of the annual lease cash flows if the opportunity cost rate is 10.0 percent annually?

    b. What is the future value of this cash flow stream at the end of Year 5 if the cash flows are invested at 10.0 percent annually? What is the present value of this future value when discounted at 10.0 percent? What does this result indicate about the consistency inherent in time value analyses?

    c. Does the office renovation and subsequent lease agreement appear to be a good investment for the company? (Hint: Compare the cost of renovation with the present value of the lease payments. Use a 10 percent discount rate for the analysis.)

7. Now assume that it is five years later and the company was unable to accumulate the $200,000 needed to make the software purchase. Instead, it is forced to borrow the $200,000. The loan calls for repayment in equal annual installments over a four-year period, with the first payment due at the end of one year. Assuming that the company can borrow the funds at a 10.0 percent rate, what amount of interest and principal will be repaid at the end of each year of the loan?

8. Throughout this case, you have been either discounting or compounding cash flows. Many financial analyses, such as bond refunding decisions, capital investment decisions, and lease decisions, involve discounting projected future cash flows. What is the appropriate rate in such situations? What factors influence the value of this rate?

UNIVERSITY MEDICAL FOUNDATION, INC.
FINANCIAL RISK

12

University Medical Foundation (UMF), Inc., is a not-for-profit corporation formed by physicians in the College of Medicine at Southeastern University. UMF, with over 600 physicians, provides the medical staff for University Hospital. In addition, UMF staffs and administers a network of 25 ambulatory care clinics and centers at ten locations within 50 miles of the hospital. In 2002, UMF generated over $500 million in revenues from about 40,000 inpatient stays and 750,000 outpatient visits.

Over 70 percent of UMF's revenues currently come from inpatient stays, but this percentage has been declining, and by 2005, over half of UMF's revenues are expected to stem from outpatient services. As improvements are made in technology and third-party payers continue to pressure providers to cut costs, more and more inpatient services will be converted to outpatient and home care. For example, in 1992, 80 percent of UMF's ophthalmological surgeries took place in University Hospital, while in 2002, 80 percent were conducted in outpatient settings.

Although UMF has traditionally provided only specialty services, in 1998 it instituted a "personal physician services" program, in which patients can receive both primary and specialty care from College of Medicine physicians. This was the first step in UMF's drive to develop an integrated delivery system, which offers a full range of patient services. Now that the system is in place, UMF is contracting with managed care plans to provide virtually all physician services required locally by plan members. Furthermore, UMF is examining the feasibility of contracting directly with employers, and hence bypassing managed care plans, but no decision has yet been made. Indeed, state insurance industry representatives expressed opposition to the idea when UMF first announced the possibility of direct contracting. The insurance industry position is that direct contracting with employers to provide a complete healthcare benefit package is an insurance function, which can be undertaken only by licensed insurance plans.

As part of its continuing education program, UMF holds monthly "nonclinical grand rounds" for its physicians, in which various staff members and outside specialists conduct seminars on nonclinical topics of interest. As part of this series, Chris Johnson, UMF's chief financial officer, has been invited to conduct two sessions on the financial risk inherent in integrated delivery systems. His main concern is that physicians, although very sophisticated in clinical matters, have a very limited understanding of basic financial risk concepts and will not appreciate the financial issues involved in integrated delivery systems without first gaining an understanding of basic financial risk concepts. Thus, he plans to devote the entire first session to basic concepts.

As preparation for the seminar, Chris developed the return distributions for the five investments shown in Table 12.1. To create the table he first hypothesized that there could be five possible economic states for the coming year, ranging from poor to excellent. Next, he estimated the one-year returns on each investment under each state. The five investments are (1) T-bills, (2) real asset investment Project A, (3) real asset investment Project B, (4) an index fund designed to proxy the returns on the S&P 500 stock index, and (5) an equity investment in UMF itself. T-bills are short-term (one-year or less maturity) U.S. Treasury debt securities; Project A is a proposed sports medicine clinic; and Project B is a Medicaid-funded project for providing family health services to an underserved area. Note that Chris developed the returns for Projects A and B and for UMF as a whole by assessing the impact of each economic state on healthcare utilization and reimbursement patterns.

In addition to the returns on these alternative investments, Chris developed the following questions to use as the structure for his presentation. See if you can answer his questions.

State of the Economy	Probability	Estimated Return on Investment				
		1-Year T-Bill	Project A	Project B	S&P 500 Fund	Equity in UMF
Poor	0.10	7.0%	−8.0%	18.0%	−15.0%	0.0%
Below average	0.20	7.0	2.0	23.0	0.0	5.0
Average	0.40	7.0	14.0	7.0	15.0	10.0
Above average	0.20	7.0	25.0	−3.0	30.0	15.0
Excellent	0.10	7.0	33.0	2.0	45.0	20.0

TABLE 12.1
Estimated One-Year Return Distributions on Five Investments

1. Is the return on the one-year T-bill risk free?

Suriya

2. Calculate the expected rate of return on each of the five investment alternatives listed in Table 12.1. Based solely on expected returns, which of the potential investments appears best?

3. Now calculate the standard deviations and coefficients of variation of returns for the five alternatives. (Hint: Coefficient of variation of return is defined as the standard deviation divided by the expected rate of return. It is a standardized measure of risk that assesses risk per unit of return.)
   a. What type of risk do these statistics measure?
   b. Is the standard deviation or the coefficient of variation the better measure?
   c. How do the five investment alternatives compare when risk is considered?

4. Suppose UMF forms a two-asset portfolio by investing in both Projects A and B.
   a. To begin, assume that the required investment is the same for both projects—say, $5,000,000 each.
      1. What would be the portfolio's expected rate of return, standard deviation, and coefficient of variation?
      2. How do these values compare with the corresponding values for the individual projects?

3. What characteristic of the two return distributions makes risk reduction possible?

b. What do you think would happen to the portfolio's expected rate of return and standard deviation if the portfolio contained 75 percent of Project A? If it contained 75 percent of Project B?

5. Now consider a portfolio consisting of investments in Project A and the S&P 500 Fund.

a. First, consider a portfolio containing equal investment in the two assets. Would this portfolio have the same risk-reducing effect as the Project A/ Project B portfolio considered in Question 4? Explain.

b. What are the expected returns and standard deviations for a portfolio mix of 0 percent Project A, 10 percent Project A, 20 percent Project A, and so on—up to 100 percent Project A?

6. Suppose an individual investor starts with a portfolio consisting of one randomly selected stock.

a. What would happen to the portfolio's risk if more and more randomly selected stocks were added?

b. What are the implications for investors? Do portfolio effects have an impact on the way investors should think about the riskiness of individual securities?

c. Explain the differences between stand-alone risk, diversifiable risk, and portfolio risk.

d. Suppose that you choose to hold a single stock investment in isolation. Should you expect to be compensated for all of the risk that you assume?

7. Now change Table 12.1 by crossing out the state of the economy and probability columns and replacing them with Year 1, Year 2, Year 3, Year 4, and Year 5. In other words, assume that the distributions represent historical returns earned on each asset in each of the last five years.

a. Plot four lines on a scatter diagram (regression lines) that show the returns on the S&P 500 Fund (the market) on the X axis and (1) T-bill returns, (2)

Project A returns, (3) Project B returns, and (4) UMF returns on the Y axis.

   1.   What are these lines called?

   2.   Estimate the slope coefficient of each line. What is the slope coefficient called, and what is its significance? (If you have a calculator with statistical functions or are using a spreadsheet, use linear regression to find the slope coefficients.)

   3.   What is the significance of the distance between the plot points and the regression line — that is, the errors?

b. Plot two lines on a different scatter diagram that show the returns on UMF (the company) on the X axis and (1) Project A returns and (2) Project B returns on the Y axis.

   1.   What are these lines called?

   2.   Estimate the slope coefficient of each line. What is the slope coefficient called and what is its significance? (If you have a calculator with statistical functions or are using a spreadsheet, use linear regression to find the slope coefficients.)

c. If you were an individual investor who could buy any of the assets in Table 12.1, which one(s) would you buy? Why? (Hint: To help answer this question, construct a Security Market Line graph and plot the returns on each asset on the graph. Also, note that UMF is actually a not-for-profit corporation, so it would be impossible to buy an equity interest in the company. For this question, assume that UMF were an investor-owned company.)

d. Now assume that you are the CEO of UMF and you have to decide whether to invest in Project A, Project B, or both. Which project(s) would you choose if you could accept both? If you could only accept one of the two, which would you choose? Why? (Hint: To help answer this question, construct a "Corporate Market Line" graph, which plots corporate betas rather than market betas on the X axis, and plot the returns for each project on the graph.)

MC 8. a. What is the market risk of each project (A and B) relative to the aggregate market risk of UMF? (For this question, assume that UMF were an investor-owned company.)

    b. What is the corporate risk of each project (A and B) relative to the aggregate corporate risk of UMF?

9. a. What is the efficient markets hypothesis (EMH)?

    b. What impact does this theory have on decisions concerning investments in securities?

    c. Is the EMH applicable to real asset investments such as the decision of UMF to invest in Project A or Project B?

    d. What impact does the EMH have on corporate financing decisions?

CHESAPEAKE HEALTHCARE (A)

BOND VALUATION

13

CHESAPEAKE HEALTHCARE is an investor-owned hospital chain that owns and operates nine hospitals in Delaware, Maryland, and Virginia. Marcia Long, a recent graduate of a prominent health services administration program, has just been hired by Baltimore Medical Center, Chesapeake's largest hospital. Like all new management personnel, Marcia must undergo three months of intensive indoctrination at the system level before joining the hospital.

Marcia began her indoctrination in January 2003. Her first assignment at Chesapeake was to review its latest annual report. This was a stroke of luck for Marcia because her father owned several bonds issued by Chesapeake, and Marcia was especially interested in whether or not her father had made a good investment. To glean more information about the bonds, Marcia examined Note E to Chesapeake's Consolidated Financial Statements, which lists the company's long-term debt obligations, including its first mortgage bonds, installment contracts, and term loans. Table 13.1 contains information on three of the first mortgage bonds listed in Chesapeake's annual report. (For more information on bond ratings, see Standard & Poor's web site at www.standardpoor.com or the Moody's Investors Services web site at www.moodys.com.)

Unfortunately, Chesapeake's CFO, Hugo Welsh, found out about Marcia's interest in the firm's debt financing. "Because you are so interested in our financial structure," he said, "here are some questions that

		Maturity	Years to	S&P Bond
Face Amount	Coupon Rate	Date	Maturity	Rating
$ 48,000,000	4 1/2	12/31/07	5	A+
32,000,000	8 1/4	12/13/17	15	A+
100,000,000	12 5/8	12/31/27	25	A+

TABLE 13.1
Chesapeake Healthcare:
Partial Long-Term
Bond Listing

I've developed as part of a debt financing presentation to our executive committee. See if you can answer them."

Marcia viewed Mr. Welsh's questions as a challenge, as she was convinced that she knew as much about debt financing as most finance MBAs. Apparently Marcia was right because she answered the questions with no difficulty. In fact, Mr. Welsh was so impressed that he asked Marcia to give the presentation to the executive committee, which turned out to be a big success. See if you can do as good a job as Marcia in answering the following questions:

1. To begin, refer to the three bonds listed in Table 13.1. Note that each bond matures at the end of the listed year, and the remaining term to maturity is also listed in the table. Furthermore, each bond has a $1,000 par value, each had a 30-year maturity when it was issued, and all three bonds currently have a 10 percent required nominal rate of return.

   a. Why do the bonds' coupon rates vary so widely?

   b. What would be the value of each bond if it had annual coupon payments?

   c. Chesapeake's bonds, like virtually all bonds, actually pay interest semiannually. What is each bond's value under these conditions? Are the bonds currently selling at a discount or at a premium?

   d. What is the effective annual rate of return implied by the values obtained in Part c?

   e. Would you expect a semiannual payment bond to sell at a higher or lower price than an otherwise equivalent annual payment bond? Look at the values calculated in Parts b and c for the five-year bond. Are the prices shown consistent with your expectations? Explain.

2. Now, regardless of your answers to Question 1, assume that the 5-year bond is selling for $800.00, the 15-year bond is selling for $865.49, and the 25-year bond is selling for $1,220.00. (Use these same prices, and assume semiannual coupons, for all of the remaining questions in this case.)

   a. What is the stated (as opposed to effective annual) yield to maturity (YTM) on each bond? (Note: The stated rate is also called the nominal rate.)

   b. What is the effective annual YTM on each issue?

   c. In comparing bond yields with the yields on other securities, should the stated or effective YTM be used? In comparing yields among bonds, should the stated or effective YTM be used? Explain.

   d. Explain the economic meaning of YTM.

3. Suppose Chesapeake has a second bond with 25 years left to maturity (in addition to the one listed in Table 13.1) that has a coupon rate of 7 3/8 percent and a market price of $747.48.

   a. What are (1) the stated and (2) the effective annual YTMs on this bond?

   b. What is the current yield on each of the 25-year bonds?

   c. What is each bond's expected price on January 1, 2004, and its capital gains yield for 2003, assuming no change in interest rates? (Hint: Remember that the nominal YTM on each 25-year bond, which is assumed to be its required rate of return, is 10.18 percent.)

   d. What would happen to the value (and price in an efficient market) of each bond over time? (Again, assume constant future interest rates.)

   e. What is the expected total (percentage) return on each bond during 2003?

   f. If you were a tax-paying investor, which of the two 25-year bonds would you prefer? Why? What impact would this preference have on the prices, and hence YTMs, of the two bonds?

4. Consider the riskiness of the three bonds listed in Table 13.1.

a. Explain the difference between price risk and reinvestment rate risk.

b. Which of the bonds has the most price risk? Why?

c. Assume that you bought 5-year, 15-year, and 25-year bonds, all with a 10 percent coupon rate and semiannual coupons, at their $1,000 par values. Which bond's value would be affected most if interest rates rose to 13 percent? Which would be affected least?

d. Assume that your investment horizon (or expected holding period) is 25 years. Which of the bonds listed in Table 13.1 has the greatest reinvestment rate risk? Why? Is there a type of bond you could buy to eliminate reinvestment rate risk?

e. Assume that you plan to keep your money invested, and to reinvest all interest receipts, for five years. Furthermore, assume you bought the 5-year bond for $800, and interest rates suddenly fell to 5 percent and remained at that level for five years.

   (1) Set up a timeline that can be used to calculate the actual (realized) rate of return on the bond. (Hint: Each interest receipt must be compounded to the maturity date at the reinvestment rate and then summed, along with the maturity value. Then, the rate of return that equates this terminal value to the initial price of the bond is the bond's realized rate of return.) How does your answer compare with the bond's YTM?

   (2) Suppose that interest rates had risen to 15 percent rather than fallen to 5 percent?

   (3) How would the results have differed if you had bought the 25-year bond rather than the 5-year bond?

f. Today, many bond market participants are speculators as opposed to long-term investors. If you thought interest rates were going to fall from current levels, what bond maturity would you buy to maximize short-term capital gains?

5. Now assume that the 15-year bond is callable after five years at $1,050.
   a. What is its yield to call (YTC)? (Hint: Set up the cash flows on a timeline. If the bond is called, investors will receive interest payments for five years and then receive $1,050 [$1,000 in principal and call premium of $50] at the end of five years. The YTM on this cash flow stream is the bond's YTC.)
   b. Do you think it is likely that the bond will be called? Explain.

6. Now consider another bond issued by Chesapeake that has not yet been discussed. This bond has a par value of $1,000 and pays interest once a year at a 10 percent rate. The bond has a mandatory sinking fund provision that requires the firm to redeem one-fifth of the outstanding issue in each year beginning at the end of Year 3 and continuing until the entire issue is retired at the end of Year 7. If the required rate of return on this bond is 8.0 percent, what is the current (Year 0) value of the bond?

7. Discuss the basic differences between the bonds issued by investor-owned corporations and those issued by not-for-profit healthcare organizations through municipal financing authorities.

8. Explain how investors set required rates of return on debt securities. (Hint: Think in terms of the real risk-free rate plus any risk borne by investors.)

9. What is the term structure of interest rates? What is a yield curve? Why is the yield curve important to both investors and managers?

10. Briefly describe the bond rating system, including the names of the major rating agencies, the ratings used, the criteria for assigning ratings, and the importance of ratings to both investors and managers. Also, describe the concept of credit enhancement and how issuers should evaluate whether or not to use it.

CHESAPEAKE HEALTHCARE (B)

STOCK VALUATION

14

CHESAPEAKE HEALTHCARE is an investor-owned hospital chain that owns and operates nine hospitals in Delaware, Maryland, and Virginia. Marcia Long, a recent graduate of a prominent health services administration program, has just been hired by Baltimore Medical Center, Chesapeake's largest hospital. Like all new management personnel, Marcia must undergo three months of intensive indoctrination at the system level before joining the hospital.

In Case 13, Chesapeake Healthcare (A), Marcia conducted an analysis of the firm's bonds and presented her findings to the company's executive committee. Chesapeake's CFO, Hugo Welsh, was very impressed with the quality of Marcia's presentation. Furthermore, the other members of the committee stated that they learned a great deal about debt financing from Marcia's presentation and that they would like to see a similar presentation on equity financing. Because Marcia would be leaving corporate headquarters to start her hospital assignment in less than four weeks, Mr. Welsh immediately assigned her the task of analyzing the firm's equity situation and preparing another presentation for the executive committee.

Marcia began by reexamining the firm's Annual Report to get some basic data. Then, she searched the *Wall Street Journal*, *Value Line*, and other potential sources of financial data to obtain some market data as well as analysts' forecasts for the firm. Table 14.1 contains the information that Marcia developed. (For information on thousands of stocks,

TABLE 14.1
Chesapeake Healthcare:
Selected Stock Data

Historical Data:

Year	Earnings per Share	Dividends per Share
1997	$1.14	$0.21
1998	1.32	0.32
1999	1.54	0.35
2000	1.56	0.36
2001	1.80	0.39
2002	2.00	0.48

Assumed Current (January 1, 2003) Data:

Current stock price	$8.00
Estimated dividend growth rates:	
Next 5 years	10.0%
Long-term steady state	4.0%
Market data:	
Yield on long-term Treasury bonds	5.0%
Merrill Lynch estimate of market returns	11.0%
Value Line beta coefficient	1.2

including beta estimates, see the Yahoo finance web page at biz.yahoo .com/p/. To go to healthcare stocks, click on Healthcare, which leads to a listing of four related industries. Click on one of the industries to obtain a listing of the stocks in that industry. Finally, click on one of the company names to obtain key information on that stock.)

As before, Mr. Welsh did not want Marcia to go off on a tangent, so he provided her with a list of questions to answer. Also as before, Marcia welcomed the challenge of working on a task that was traditionally assigned to finance MBAs, rather than to graduates of health services administration programs. Put yourself in Marcia's shoes and see how you would fare if assigned this task and needed to answer the following questions:

1.   a. What are Chesapeake's historical earnings and dividend growth rates over the entire 1997–2002

period? (Hint: Use 1997 data for the present values; 2002 data for the future values, and 1 as the number of periods.)

   b. What are the average annual compounded growth rates? (Hint: Use 1997 data for the present values, 2002 data for future values, and 5 as the number of periods.)

   c. Which rate (overall or annual) better expresses the concept of growth?

2. a. What was the firm's payout ratio in 2002? (Hint: The payout ratio is the percentage of earnings paid out to stockholders as dividends.)

   b. What was Chesapeake's average payout over the past six years?

   c. If the payout ratio of an average investor-owned hospital company were about 50 percent, is Chesapeake's payout about average, below average, or above average? What is the primary factor that influences a business's payout ratio?

3. a. What is the Capital Asset Pricing Model (CAPM)? What is the Security Market Line (SML)?

   b. Graph the SML using the data presented in Table 14.1.

   c. What would happen to the SML if investors' risk aversion increased and the required rate of return on the market rose to 12 percent?

   d. What would happen to the SML if inflation expectations increased by 1 percentage point? (Hint: Investors would add 1 percentage point to their required rates of return on all assets, including risk-free assets.)

   e. Return to the base case data in Part b of this question. According to the SML, what is the required rate of return on Chesapeake's stock? Plot that point on your SML graph.

4. Assume that analysts estimated that Chesapeake would have a long-term (constant) dividend growth rate of 5.0 percent. Furthermore, Table 14.1 gives a 2002 dividend (D_o) of $0.48 and an end of year

(December 31, 2002, or January 1, 2003) stock price (P_o) of $8.

    a. What is the expected rate of return on Chesapeake's stock if it was purchased on January 1, 2003?

    b. What is the expected dividend yield and expected capital gains yield?

    c. What is the relationship between dividend yield and capital gains yield over time under constant growth assumptions?

    d. What conditions must hold to use the constant growth model? Do many "real-world" stocks satisfy the constant growth assumptions?

    e. Plot the expected rate of return found in Part a on the SML graph from Question 3. Based on the data developed so far, would you buy Chesapeake's stock?

5. Now consider the fact that *Value Line* actually predicted that Chesapeake's dividends would grow at a 10 percent rate for the next five years, and then the growth rate would fall to a steady state (constant) 4 percent into the foreseeable future.

    a. Under these conditions, what is the value of Chesapeake's stock at the beginning of 2003? (Hint: Lay out the expected dividends on a time line up to and including the first year of constant [4 percent] growth. Use the dividend expected in Year 6 and the constant growth model to calculate the value of the stock at the end of Year 5. Discount this Year 5 value, along with the dividends expected in Years 1–5 back to Year 0. Sum these present values to obtain the value of the stock.)

    b. Assume that the value you calculated was the actual stock price on January 1, 2003. What is the expected stock price at the end of 2003 assuming that the stock is in equilibrium?

    c. What are the expected dividend yield, capital gains yield, and total return for 2003?

d. Repeat the Part c analysis for 2004. What happens to the expected dividend and capital gains yields from 2003 to 2004? What are the expected dividend and capital gains yields for 2008?

6. Chesapeake's stock price was actually $8.00 at the beginning of 2003. Using the growth rates given in Table 14.1 (and also used in Question 5), what is the stock's expected rate of return? (Hint: This is not an easy question. A model similar to the one used to answer Question 5 must be applied, but a trial-and-error technique must be used to find the discount rate that discounts the expected dividend [and Year 5 stock value] stream back to the current price, $8.00. The process is complicated by the fact that each discount rate selected in the trial-and-error process must be used to find the Year 5 stock value before it is used to discount the expected cash flow stream back to Year 0.)

7. What is the efficient markets hypothesis and what are its implications for stock investors?

Capital
Acquisition

GOLD COAST HOMECARE

COST OF CAPITAL

15

GOLD COAST HOMECARE was founded in 1982 in Miami, Florida as a taxable partnership by Maria Gonzalez, M.D., Ramon Garcia, R.N., and Bruce Vogel, L.P.T. Its purpose was to provide an "at-home" alternative to hospitals and ambulatory care facilities for basic healthcare services provided by physicians, registered nurses, licensed practical nurses, and physical therapists. (For more information on home health services, see the web site of the National Association for Home Care [NAHC] at www.nahc.org.)

The partnership enjoyed enormous success from the very first day. Even its founders were surprised at how easy it was to establish and run the business. The founding coincided with the search by third-party payers for alternative, and potentially less costly, delivery settings. Also, the AIDS epidemic provided a patient clientele that was totally unexpected. On the basis of their success in metropolitan Miami, the partnership expanded services into Fort Lauderdale and West Palm Beach, and then moved into other metropolitan areas in Florida and across the Southeast. They also expanded their services at each location to include occupational, speech, and rehabilitation therapies.

The founders had sufficient personal resources to start the company, and they had enough confidence in the business plan to commit most of their own funds to the new venture. However, after only six years, the external capital requirements brought on by rapid growth exhausted their personal funds, and they were forced to borrow heavily.

Soon, although they still needed external capital to finance growth, the partnership's ability to borrow at reasonable rates was exhausted. Thus, in 1992 they incorporated the partnership, and in 1995 they sold common stock to the public through an initial public offering (IPO). The founders still retain a large, but minority, ownership position in the company, and currently the stock trades in the over-the-counter market, although there has been some talk of listing on a regional exchange.

Gold Coast is widely recognized as one of the regional leaders in its industry, and it won an award in 1998 for being one of the 100 best-managed small companies in the United States. The company has two operating divisions: (1) the Healthcare Services Division and (2) the Information Systems Division. The Healthcare Services Division operates Gold Coast's home health care services at the company's 22 locations. Because sales and earnings in this division are relatively predictable, the business risk of this division is about average.

The Information Systems Division sells the computer software system that Gold Coast designed to control its own operations to other home health care companies. This system combines inventory control, visit scheduling, clinical record keeping, billing and collections, and payroll into a single integrated package. Although the system is excellent, this division competes head to head with several major software firms as well as with information services and management consulting firms. Because of this competition, and the rapid technological changes inherent in the information services industry, Gold Coast's management considers the Information Services Division to have more business risk than the Healthcare Services Division.

Although the company's growth has been exceptional, it has been more random than planned. The founders would simply decide on a location for a new office, run an advertisement in a local newspaper for clinical professionals and clerical employees, send in an experienced manager from one of the established offices, and begin to make money almost immediately. Formal decision structures were almost nonexistent, but the company's head start and its bright, energetic founders easily overcame any deficiencies in its managerial decision-making processes.

However, recent changes in the market for home health care services portend a much more difficult environment in the future. First, until recently, relatively generous payment amounts for home health care services have produced intense competition. Other investor-owned home health care firms have sprung up like weeds, especially in major cities, and several hospitals in Gold Coast's service area, including not-for-profits, have begun to offer home health care services. Second, the rapid increase in expenditures on home health care services has prompted payers to drastically reduce reimbursement amounts, just as new capacity came on line. In particular, the Balanced Budget Act of 1997 mandated lower payment amounts for Medicare home health services beginning in October 1997. Initially, this was accomplished through a cost-based interim payment system (IPS), which was then replaced on October 1, 2000, by a totally new prospective payment system (PPS). (For more information on this system, see www.hcfa.gov/medicare/hhmain.htm.)

Because of these changes, Gold Coast's board of directors has concluded that the company must start to apply state-of-the-art techniques in both its operations and its corporate managerial processes. As a first step, the board has directed the financial vice president to develop an estimate for the company's cost of capital. The financial VP, in turn, has directed Gold Coast's treasurer, Clark Ruffin, to prepare and submit a cost of capital estimate in two weeks. Clark has an accounting background, and his primary task since taking over as treasurer has been cash and short-term liability management. Thus, he is somewhat apprehensive about his new assignment, an apprehension that is heightened by the fact that one of the board members is a well-regarded University of Florida finance professor.

Clark began by reviewing Gold Coast's 2002 financial statements, which are presented in Table 15.1 in simplified form. Next, he assembled the following data:

1. Gold Coast's long-term debt consists of 7 percent coupon, BBB-rated, semiannual payment bonds with 15 years remaining to maturity. The bonds recently traded at a price of $913.54 per $1,000 par value bond. The bonds are callable in five years at par value plus a call premium of one year's interest, for a total of $1,100.

    contributes to WACC

2. The founders have an aversion to short-term debt, so the company uses such debt only to fund cyclical

TABLE 15.1
Gold Coast Homecare:
2002 Financial
Statement Extracts
(millions of dollars)

Balance Sheet:

Cash and marketable securities	$ 2.5	Accounts payable	$ 1.1
Accounts receivable	5.9	Accruals	1.0
Inventory	1.3	Notes payable	0.2
Current assets	$ 9.7	Current liabilities	$ 2.3
Net fixed assets	32.9	Long-term debt	20.0
		Common stock	20.3
Total assets	$42.6	Total claims	$42.6

Income Statement:

Net revenues	$80.6
Cash expenses	71.8
Depreciation	2.8
Taxable income	$ 6.0
Taxes	2.4
Net income	$ 3.6
Dividends	1.8
Additions to retained earnings	$ 1.8

bonds contribute to wacc

working capital needs. The company's financial plan calls for the issue of 30-year bonds to meet long-term debt needs.

3. Gold Coast's federal-plus-state tax rate is 40 percent.

4. Gold Coast's last dividend (D_o) was $0.18, and most analysts predict the company's dividend to grow at a relatively constant annual rate somewhere in the range of 8 to 12 percent. Gold Coast's common stock now sells at a price of $5 per share. The company has 10.0 million common shares outstanding.

5. Over the last few years, Gold Coast has averaged a 20 percent return on equity (ROE) and has paid out about 50 percent of its net income as dividends.

6. The current yield curve on U.S. Treasury securities is as follows:

Term to Maturity	Yield
3 months	2.5%
6 months	3.0
9 months	3.3
1 year	3.5
5 years	4.0
10 years	4.4
15 years	4.7
20 years	4.9
25 years	5.0
30 years	5.1

7. A prominent investment banking firm has recently estimated the expected rate of return on the S&P 500 Index to be 12.0 percent.

8. Gold Coast's historical beta, as measured by several analysts who follow the stock, falls in the range of 1.1 to 1.3.

9. The required rate of return on an average (A-rated, beta = 1.0) company's long-term debt is 7.0 percent.

10. Gold Coast's market value target capital structure calls for 35 percent long-term debt and 65 percent common stock.

11. Clark is aware of a third method (in addition to the capital asset pricing and discounted cash flow models) for estimating a firm's cost of equity: the bond yield plus risk-premium method. Here, a risk premium is added to the firm's own before-tax cost of debt estimate to obtain an estimate of the cost of equity. Note that the risk premium used here is not the market risk premium, which is applied to the risk-free rate. Rather, the risk premium reflects the difference between an average firm's cost of equity and its cost of debt.

12. About 60 percent of Gold Coast's operating assets are used by the Healthcare Services Division, and 40 percent by the Information Systems Division. Management's best estimate of the beta of its Healthcare Services Division is 1.0.

TABLE 15.2
Selected Not-for-Profit
Hospital Data

Average Long-Term Capital Structure:

30 percent debt

70 percent equity (fund capital)

Average Cost of Debt:

Interest rate on A-rated tax-exempt bonds = 4.0%

Assume that Clark has hired you as a consultant to develop Gold Coast's overall corporate cost of capital. You will have to meet with the financial VP and, possibly, with the president and the full board of directors (including the founders and the finance professor) to present your findings and answer any questions they might have.

Recently, the divisional presidents have expressed concern that a single cost of capital will be applied across the company, regardless of any divisional risk differences. Clark has asked you to be sure to address their concerns. Specifically, he wants you to develop divisional costs of capital in addition to the overall corporate cost of capital.

Additionally, the founders of Gold Coast are very concerned about the threat posed by home health care businesses started by not-for-profit hospitals because they have both cost (in the sense that they do not pay dividends) and tax advantages. To help assess the threat, Clark has asked you to use the information developed for Gold Coast, along with the not-for-profit hospital data contained in Table 15.2, to estimate the cost of capital for an average not-for-profit hospital's home health care business.

Finally, one of Gold Coast's directors has expressed concern over the difference between the company's target capital structure and the current structure as reported on the balance sheet. Clark wondered if this should be a matter of concern. (Hint: Think about book values versus market values.)

Optional information: If you are familiar with the marginal cost of capital concept, which recognizes flotation costs by differentiating between the cost of retained earnings and the cost of new common stock, you may want to prepare the marginal cost of capital schedule for Gold Coast, but not for its divisions. To make this estimate, assume total equity flotation costs (including underwriting, signaling, and market pressure costs) of 30 percent and a retained earnings estimate of $2 million and a depreciation expense estimate of $3 million for the Year 2003.)

MEDICAL TEMPS, INC.

CAPITAL STRUCTURE
ANALYSIS

16

MEDICAL TEMPS, INC., franchises "rent-a-nurse" businesses to independent operators throughout the United States. The concept of the business is the same as other temporary help services, such as Manpower and Kelly Temporary Services, except that Medical Temps deals only with registered nurses. (For more information on franchising, see the American Franchisee Association web site at www.franchisee.org.)

The rationale behind Medical Temps is as follows:

1. Many healthcare providers, especially hospitals, have difficulty hiring and retaining nurses, so there is almost always a demand for nursing professionals. Hospitals are the largest employer of registered nurses, employing almost 60 percent of the roughly 2.7 million working nurses. Traditionally, hospitals have been the dominant employer of nurses, but now nurses have opportunities that weren't even dreamed of a generation ago. Registered nurses can work as nurse practitioners, nurse anesthetists, or critical-care or neonatal specialists, all of which are in high demand today. In addition, they can work in home health agencies, nursing homes, utilization review positions, physicians' offices or outpatient surgery centers, and in a multitude of other nonhospital settings such as schools. Of all the work settings, hospitals are generally considered

TABLE 16.1
Average Annual
Income of Registered
Nurses

Position	Annual Income
Acute care	$45,000
Ambulatory care	44,000
Nurse manager	65,000
Nurse practitioner	62,000
Operating room	45,000
Physician's office	36,500
National average	45,000

Source: Allied Physicians web site, www.allied-physicians.com.

to be the least desirable because of the hard work, rigid work conditions, and irregular working hours. (For more information about the nursing profession, see the American Nurses Association web site at www.nursingworld.org.)

2. Providers are very reluctant to build a large base of fixed costs, so any staffing requirements that may not be permanent in nature are often filled by temporary workers. Also, when vacancies occur among permanent workers, providers often need temporary nurses to carry the load until the vacancies are filled with permanent personnel.

3. Although nursing salaries have increased over the past ten years (see Table 16.1), real wages have barely kept up with inflation. Furthermore, a large number of nurses have quit the profession for a variety of reasons, including family responsibilities. Many of these nurses are willing to work occasionally but not on a permanent basis.

4. Typically, the nurses who want to work on a selective basis have spouses who provide family coverage health insurance. Also, these nurses do not require extensive fringe benefits such as pension plans or paid vacations, and because they are part-time workers, they are not

eligible for unemployment insurance or workers' compensation. Thus, if the average fringe-benefit package paid for permanent nurses is, say, 25 percent of salary, a temporary services company could offer a salary to its nurses 5 percent higher than can providers; could "rent" the nurses out at 5 percent less than it costs providers to hire permanent nurses, including all fringe benefits; and could pocket what remains of the 15 percent spread after administrative costs are paid. Note, however, that the actual rates charged by Medical Temp's franchisees are related more to local supply and demand conditions than to costs.

Franchisees buy the exclusive right to use the Medical Temps name within a specified territory from Medical Temps, the franchisor. In addition, franchisees receive marketing and management support from Medical Temps as well as the right to lease computers and other office equipment under relatively favorable terms. Finally, franchisees can purchase expendable office supplies directly from Medical Temps at substantial savings from retail prices.

To start operations, a franchisee recruits a pool of nurses from the local labor market. Then, when a client needs a temporary nurse, the local manager matches the client's specific needs with a qualified nurse from the pool. The bill for services is sent to the client by the franchisee based on the number of hours—verified by a timecard—that the nurse works for the client. The client has no responsibility for the nurse's salary or fringe benefits; this is all handled by the Medical Temps franchisee.

Tiffany Radcliff, a registered nurse from Albuquerque who left the profession to get an MBA from the University of New Mexico, founded Medical Temps in 1985. The firm grew rapidly from its base in Albuquerque, first by expanding operations into different cities across the Southwest and then by franchising into other parts of the country. Tiffany was a devout believer in the virtues of equity financing. Although the firm had issued debt periodically, especially to finance company-owned business expansion, Tiffany always used the firm's free cash flow to retire the debt as soon as possible. Recent growth has involved franchising, in which the franchisee puts up the required capital, and hence there has been no need for outside capital for several years.

Tiffany believes that her firm's high-growth days are over. First, numerous companies that offer competing services have appeared on the scene. Second, the number of hospitals, which are her primary clients, has actually declined over the years since she founded the firm and a meaningful increase in hospital beds is unlikely in the foreseeable future. Third, some hospitals are creating "flexible staffing pools" for nurses that, for all practical purposes, are in-house temporary work agencies. Finally, many large employers of nurses are recruiting internationally, which lessens the demand for temporary workers. Thus, Tiffany expects the firm's earnings before interest and taxes (EBIT) to grow relatively slowly in the future.

Medical Temps has 10 million shares of common stock outstanding, which are traded in the over-the-counter market. The current share price is $1.20, so the total market value of the firm's equity is $12 million. The book value of equity is also $12 million, so the stock now sells at its book value. The firm's federal-plus-state tax rate is 40 percent. Tiffany owns 20 percent of the outstanding stock, and others in the management group own an additional 10 percent.

Tiffany's financial manager, Paul Duncan, has been preaching for years that Medical Temps should use debt in its capital structure. "After all," says Paul, "everybody else uses debt, and some of our competitors use over 50 percent debt financing. Also, an underleveraged company is exposed to a hostile takeover because raiders can use the firm's excess debt capacity to finance the bid."

If the firm were to recapitalize, the borrowed funds would be used to repurchase stock in the open market, as the funds are not needed to support growth. Tiffany's reaction to Paul's prodding is cautious, but she is willing to give Paul the chance to prove his point. Paul has worked with Tiffany for the past six years and knows that the only way he can convince her that the firm should use debt financing is to conduct a comprehensive analysis.

To begin, Paul arranged for a joint meeting with an investment banker who specializes in corporate financing for service companies. After several hours, the pair agreed on the estimates for the relationships between the use of debt financing and Medical Temps' capital costs shown in Table 16.2. Additionally, Paul obtained industry capitalization data for companies that franchise professional services along with the matching debt ratings on the basis of rough guidance given by Standard & Poor's Ratings Services. These data are contained in Table 16.3.

Amount Borrowed	Cost of Debt	Cost of Equity
$ 0	—	15.0%
2,500,000	10.0%	15.5
5,000,000	11.0	16.5
7,500,000	13.0	18.0
10,000,000	16.0	20.0
12,500,000	20.0	25.0

TABLE 16.2
Relationships Between the Level of Debt Financing and Capital Costs

Percentile	Market Value Debt Ratio	Debt Rating
10th	10%	AAA
25th	25	AA
40th	35	A
Median	50	BBB
60th	65	BB
75th	75	B
90th	82	C

Note: The debt ratio is defined as Total debt/Total assets.

TABLE 16.3
Industry Average Data and Matching Debt Ratings

Although Medical Temps' EBIT is expected to be $3 million in 2003, there is some uncertainty in the estimate, as indicated by the following probability distribution:

Probability	EBIT
0.25	$2,500,000
0.50	3,000,000
0.25	3,500,000

On the basis of previous conversations, Paul knows that Tiffany has two major concerns regarding the use of debt financing. First, she is concerned about the impact of debt financing on the firm's reported profitability; that is, the impact of debt financing on net income and ROE as reported in the firm's financial statements. Furthermore, any risk implications to stockholders must be identified. To help in this regard, Paul plans to construct partial income statements (beginning with EBIT) for four levels of debt as measured by the book value Total debt/Total assets ratio: zero, 25 percent, 50 percent, and 75 percent. For this analysis, which will not be used to make the actual capital structure decision, Paul intends to use a cost of debt of 10 percent regardless of the amount of debt financing used.

In addition to accounting effects, Tiffany is obviously concerned about the potential impact of debt financing on the firm's shareholders: specifically, what impact debt financing will have on stock price. To help address this issue, Paul is aware of a technique that can be used to value zero-growth firms at different debt levels. Clearly, the results of this analysis do not apply exactly to Medical Temps, which is expected to experience slow growth, as opposed to zero growth, over the coming years. Here are the equations used in the analysis:

$$E = [EBIT - (R(R_d) \times D)](1 - T)/R(R_e). \tag{1}$$

$$V = E + D. \tag{2}$$

$$P = (V - D_0)/n_0. \tag{3}$$

$$n_1 = n_0 - D/P. \tag{4}$$

In these equations,

E = market value of equity.

$EBIT$ = earnings before interest and taxes.

$R(R_d)$ = cost of debt.

D = market (and book) value of new debt.

D_0 = market value of old debt.

T = tax rate.

$R(R_e)$ = cost of equity.

V = total market value.

P = stock price after recapitalization.

n_0 = number of shares before recapitalization.

n_1 = number of shares after recapitalization.

Paul is also concerned about potential changes in the healthcare industry and how they might affect the basic business risk of Medical Temps. Table 16.4 contains leverage/cost estimates at alternative business risk levels.

Significant Increase in Business Risk:

Amount Borrowed	Cost of Debt	Cost of Equity
$ 0	—	16.0%
2,500,000	11.0%	17.0
5,000,000	13.0	19.0
7,500,000	16.0	22.0
10,000,000	20.0	26.0
12,500,000	25.0	31.0

Significant Decrease in Business Risk:

Amount Borrowed	Cost of Debt	Cost of Equity
$ 0	—	14.0%
2,500,000	9.0%	14.3
5,000,000	9.5	15.0
7,500,000	10.5	16.0
10,000,000	12.5	17.5
12,500,000	15.5	20.0

TABLE 16.4
Level of Debt and Cost Estimates at Different Business Risk Levels

1. The average healthcare franchise business has a times interest earned (TIE) ratio of 4.0.

2. Medical Temps, Inc. has a current cash and marketable securities balance of $500,000. The average healthcare franchise business has cash and marketable securities on hand that is equal to 70 percent of its annual interest payment.

TABLE 16.5
Additional Data

Finally, because the capital structure decision is heavily influenced by a host of qualitative factors as well as the actions of other businesses in the industry, Paul uncovered the additional industry data contained in Table 16.5.

Optional information: (Address this issue only if you are familiar with the following capital structure models.) Paul knows that Tiffany is familiar with capital structure theory and will want to know the value of the firm according to the Modigliani-Miller (MM) with corporate taxes model and the Miller model. Because most of the other board members are not very familiar with capital structure decisions, it will be necessary to conduct a tutorial on the issues involved, including the difference between business and financial risk, the relationship between capital structure and EPS, and the additional qualitative factors that influence the decision. To ease comparisons, assume that the value of an unlevered firm is $12 million in both models. Also, assume that the personal tax rates are 25 percent on stock income and 30 percent on debt income.

M. D. PETERSON CANCER CENTER
LEASING DECISIONS

17

M. D. PETERSON CANCER CENTER (the Center) is an internationally known not-for-profit inpatient and outpatient facility dedicated to the prevention and treatment of cancer. Specific treatment services include surgery, chemotherapy, bone marrow transplantation, radiation therapy, and photodynamic therapy.

For the past ten years, the Center has been working diligently to perfect noninvasive brain surgery techniques. One technique, Gamma Knife radiosurgery, was developed in the 1950s and 1960s by Dr. Lars Leksell, a prominent Swedish neurosurgeon. The first patient treatment site was opened in 1968 in Stockholm, while the first site in the United States was established in Pittsburgh in 1977.

The Gamma Knife uses 201 separate radiation sources to treat certain brain cancers. Each of the radiation beams is quite weak, and hence does not damage normal brain tissue, but when the separate beams are focused on a single point by a collimator helmet, the Gamma Knife delivers a dosage sufficient to be highly effective. The Gamma Knife is especially useful in the treatment of arteriovenous malformations, but it can also be used to treat certain types of benign tumors and even some small malignant lesions. The primary clinical benefit of the Gamma Knife is the significant reduction in the risk associated with traditional surgical procedures, in which the morbidity and mortality rate is substantial, especially for patients with deep lesions. In addition to treating cancer, the Gamma Knife can be used to treat functional disorders such as Parkinson's disease tremors and the pain that results from trigeminal neuralgia. (For more information about the Gamma Knife, see the manufacturer's web site at www.elekta.com.)

The procedure calls for a team approach including a neurosurgeon, radiation physicist, radiologist, and radiation therapist. The neurosurgeon selects the patients appropriate for the procedure and performs the stereotactic process required to localize the target area. The radiation physicist works with a computer program to compute the appropriate dosimetry, while the radiologist performs a CT scan, MRI scan, angiogram, or a combination of the three to help the neurosurgeon localize the lesion.

The dosimetry calculations are especially complex. Because differing thicknesses of skull and brain will attenuate the beams in varying amounts, the amount of radiation applied is highly dependent on where the lesion is located and the size and shape of the patient's skull. The actual application of the radiation generally takes between 20 minutes and 2 hours, and the patient is generally released after only a short period of observation.

The Center plans to acquire a new Gamma Knife to replace its current model. The equipment has an invoice price of $3,000,000, including delivery and installation charges, and it falls into the modified accelerated cost recovery system (MACRS) five-year class, with current allowances of 0.20, 0.32, 0.19, 0.12, 0.11, and 0.06 in Years 1–6, respectively. The manufacturer of the equipment will provide a maintenance contract for $90,000 per year, payable at the beginning of each year, if the Center buys the equipment. Furthermore, the purchase could be financed by a four-year simple interest conventional (taxable) bank note that would carry an interest rate of 8 percent.

Regardless of whether the equipment is purchased or leased, the Center's managers do not think that it will be used for more than four years, at which time the Center plans to open a new radiation therapy facility. Land on which to construct a larger facility has already been acquired, and the building should be ready for occupancy at that time. The new facility is designed to enable the Center to use several new radiosurgery procedures. Thus, the Gamma Knife replacement is viewed as a "bridge" to serve only until the new facility is ready four years from now. The expected physical life of the equipment is ten years, but medical equipment of this nature is subject to unpredictable technological obsolescence.

After considerable debate among the Center's managers, they concluded that there is a 25 percent probability that the residual (salvage) value after four years will be $500,000, a 50 percent probability that it will be $1,000,000, and a 25 percent probability that it will be $2,000,000, which makes the residual value quite risky. However, the managers are not sure which residual value estimate should be used in the base case analysis: the most likely value of $1,000,000 or the expected value of $1,125,000. If the residual value is judged to have high risk, the Center's normal procedure is to apply a 5 percentage point risk adjustment to the base discount rate used on the other lease analysis flows to obtain the appropriate rate for the residual value flows.

GB Financing (GBF), a leasing company that is partially owned by the manufacturer, has presented an initial offer to the Center to lease the equipment for annual payments of $680,000, with the first payment due on delivery and installation and additional payments due at the beginning of each succeeding year of the four-year lease term. (For more information on leasing, see the Association for Equipment Leasing and Finance web site at www.elaonline.com.) This rental price includes a service contract under which the equipment would be maintained in good working order. GBF would buy the equipment from the manufacturer under the same terms that were offered to the Center, and GBF would have to enter into a maintenance contract with the manufacturer for $90,000 per year.

Unlike the Center, GBF forecasts a $1,500,000 residual value. Its estimate is based on the following facts: (1) There is no technology on the horizon that would make the Gamma Knife obsolete; (2) the equipment has a physical life estimated to be two and one-half times longer than the four-year lease term; and (3) GBF is more skilled in selling used equipment, especially Gamma Knives, than is the Center. GBF's federal-plus-state tax rate is 40 percent and, if the lease is not written, GBF could invest the funds in a four-year term loan of similar risk yielding 8.0 percent before taxes.

Randall Williams, the Center's CFO, has the final say on all of the business's lease-versus-purchase decisions, but the actual analysis of the relevant data will be conducted by the Center's capital funds manager, Vanessa Seagle. In the past, Randall and Vanessa have more or less agreed on analytical methodologies, but in discussing this lease analysis, they ended up in a heated discussion about the appropriate discount rate to use in calculating the present values of the cash flows.

Randall argued that the cash flows associated with performing stereotactic radiosurgery are very uncertain. He is convinced that insurers are not going to be nearly as generous in the future as they have been in the past in funding such procedures, so the revenue stream is highly speculative. Furthermore, the negative influence of managed care plans on reimbursement rates could be accelerating in the future. Accordingly, he thinks that a high discount rate should be used in the analysis. Vanessa, on the other hand, believes that leasing is a substitute for other "financing," which means a blend of debt and equity capital. Consequently, she believes that the lease analysis cash flows should be discounted at the Center's corporate cost of capital, 10 percent. In addition to the discount rate dispute, there is also some disagreement about how the lease would be handled on the Center's financial statements, so that has to be resolved.

Both Randall and Vanessa believe that lessees should not blindly accept the first offer made by potential lessors but should conduct a complete analysis from the viewpoint of both parties, and then, using this knowledge, negotiate the best deal possible. Thus, knowing the range of lease payments that is acceptable to both parties is important.

There is a possibility that the Center will move to its new radiation facility earlier than anticipated, and hence prior to the expiration of the lease. Furthermore, if the neurosurgeon that is the primary user of this procedure leaves the staff and is not immediately replaced, the equipment would be useless. Thus, Randall is considering asking GBF to include a cancellation clause in the lease contract. Under such a clause, the Center would be able to return the equipment to GBF at any time during the lease term after giving a minimum two weeks notice. Before negotiations begin, the Center must assess the impact of such a clause on the riskiness of the lease to both parties, and any consequences that it might have on the terms of the lease.

In addition to a cancellation clause, Randall is aware that many lessors are now writing per-procedure leases, in which the lease payment is based on the number of procedures performed rather than a fixed amount. GBF has been writing such leases on terms of $7,500 to $9,500 per procedure. He wonders whether the Center might be better off negotiating for this type of lease, and what the consequences would be for both the lessee and lessor.

There also has been some discussion about obtaining tax-exempt financing for the Gamma Knife should it be purchased. If so, the cost of tax-exempt (municipal) debt would be only 5 percent. To complicate matters even more, the Center currently has over $5,000,000 in excess funds invested in marketable securities earning 3 percent, and these funds, rather than debt financing, could be used to purchase the equipment.

Finally, Randall's brother-in-law, who works at GBF, found out that GBF would probably obtain a $1,500,000 simple interest loan that it would use to leverage the lease. The terms of this loan have not been finalized, but the bank has indicated that the interest rate would be in the range of 7 to 9 percent. Such leveraging could affect the Center's ability to negotiate lower lease payments, so it is important to understand the impact of leveraging from the perspectives of both the lessee and the lessor.

Assume that you have been hired as a consultant to recommend a course of action for the Gamma Knife acquisition. Prepare a report that both addresses all of the issues raised by the parties involved and makes a final recommendation regarding the acquisition.

WAVERLY ENTERPRISES

BOND REFUNDING

18

WAVERLY ENTERPRISES is a leading provider of post-acute health-care. It is a for-profit corporation that operates over 500 skilled nursing facilities, 30 assisted living centers, 150 outpatient rehabilitation therapy clinics, and 50 hospice and home care centers. Aram Dobalian, financial VP of Waverly Enterprises, is reviewing the minutes of the company's final 2002 board of directors meeting. The major topic discussed at the meeting was whether Waverly should refund any of its currently outstanding bond issues. Of particular interest is a $100 million bond issue sold approximately five years ago carrying an 8.0 percent coupon rate. Several of the board members had taken markedly different positions on the question, and at the conclusion of the meeting the chairman of the board asked Aram to prepare a report analyzing the alternative points of view. (For more information on bonds, see the Investing in Bonds web site at www.investinginbonds.com or the Bonds Online site at www.bondsonline.com.)

The bonds in question, which are rated single-A, were issued in January 1998 when interest rates were higher than today. Issuing the bonds at that time was necessary because Waverly needed the capital to expand its rehabilitation services business line. Now, almost five years later, with lower rates, Waverly can sell A-rated bonds that carry a lower interest rate than that set on the 1998 issue.

Because Aram wanted to have flexibility regarding when the 1998 issue could be retired, he had insisted that the bonds be made callable after five years. (If the bonds had not been callable, Waverly Enterprises would have had to pay an interest rate of only 7.3 percent, 70 basis points less than the actual 8.0 percent coupon rate. If the bonds had been immediately callable, rather than having a deferred call, the coupon rate would have had to be pegged at 8.2 percent.) The bonds can be called on January 1, 2003 (the end of Year 5), but an initial call premium of one year's interest payment, or $80 per bond, would have to be paid. This premium declines by $8.0\%/25 = 0.32$ percentage points, or $3.20, each year. Thus, if the bonds were called on January 1, 2008 (the end of Year 10), the call premium would be $(8.0\%/25)(20) = 6.4\%$, or $64, where "20" represents the number of years remaining to maturity. The flotation costs on this issue amounted to 1.5 percent of the face amount, or $1,500,000. Waverly's federal-plus-state tax rate is 40 percent.

Aram estimates that Waverly currently could sell a new issue of 25-year A-rated bonds at an interest rate of 7.0 percent. The call of the old and sale of the new bonds could take place five to seven weeks after the decision to refund has been made; this time is required to give legal notice to bondholders and to arrange the financing needed to redeem the current issue. The flotation cost on the refunding issue would be 1 percent of the new issue's face amount, and funds from the new issue would be available from the underwriters the day they were needed to pay off the old bonds.

Aram had proposed at the last directors' meeting that the company call the 8.0 percent bonds at first opportunity and replace them with a new, lower coupon rate issue. Although the refunding cost would be substantial, he believed the interest savings of 100 basis points per year for 25 years on a $100 million issue would be well worth the cost. Aram did not anticipate adverse reactions from any of the board members; however, three of them voiced strong reservations about his refunding proposal.

The first was Pamela Mathias, a long-term member of Waverly Enterprises' board and chairman of Mathias & Company, an investment banking house that caters primarily to institutional clients such as insurance companies and pension funds. Pamela argued that calling the bonds for refunding would not be well received by the major institutions that hold Waverly's outstanding bonds. According to Pamela, the institutional investors who hold the bonds purchased them on the expectation of receiving the 8.0 percent interest rate for at least ten years, and these investors would be made very unhappy by a call after only five years. Because most of the leading institutions hold some of Waverly Enterprises' bonds and because the firm typically sells new bonds to finance its growth every four or five years, it would be most unfortunate if institutional investors developed a feeling of ill will toward the company.

A second director, Vincent Marchiano, who is a relatively new member of the board and president of a local bank, also opposed the call, but for an entirely different reason. Vincent believed that the decline in interest rates was not yet over. He said a study by his bank suggested that the long-term interest rate on A-rated corporate bonds might fall to 6.0 percent next year. Under questioning from the other board members, however, Vincent admitted that the interest rate decline could in fact be over and that interest rates might begin to move back up again. When pressed, Vincent produced the following probability distribution that the bank's economists had developed for interest rates on A-rated corporate bonds one year from now (January 1, 2004):

Probability	Interest Rate on A-Rated Corporate Bonds
0.10	4.0%
0.20	5.0
0.40	6.0
0.20	7.0
0.10	8.0

The board agreed that any analysis of the impact of prospective interest rates on the refunding decision would assume that Waverly would issue a 24-year bond if the refunding occurred one year hence.

The third director, Kim Mitchell, noted that interest rates had been quite volatile lately, and that if rates rose before the new issue could be sold, but after the firm had committed to the refunding, the refunding would be a disaster. Therefore, she wondered how much interest rates could increase before Waverly Enterprises lost on the refunding. Indeed, the sensitivity of the refunding NPV to current interest rate levels would be a valuable tool in making the refunding decision.

Another bond that Waverly Enterprises is considering refunding is a $25 million, 30-year issue sold about 25 years ago in January 1978. At the time this bond was issued, Waverly was in poor financial condition and was considered to be a relatively poor credit risk. To raise the $25 million, Waverly was forced to issue subordinated debentures with a B rating and a coupon rate of 11.3 percent, which was quite high at the time. The flotation cost on this issue was 2 percent of the face amount, or $500,000. This issue is callable, with five-year call protection, and the call premium is determined in the same manner as on the 1998 bond discussed earlier. Aram estimates that Waverly could refund this $25 million issue with a 25-year, 10.5 percent coupon subordinated debenture that would require a flotation cost of $250,000. Assume that this $25 million of capital will be needed for an indefinite period, so whether the bond is refunded now or in five years, it will subsequently be refunded every 25 years, with each successive replacement bond remaining outstanding to its maturity. This refunding situation also must be analyzed, but the situation differs from the first bond in that the new bond has a maturity that differs from the remaining maturity of the existing bond. (Hint: The lower part of the spreadsheet model handles this situation, but new input values must be entered to match this new refunding situation.)

Another issue of consequence to the refunding decision involves tax rates. Waverly's marginal tax rate could fall from its current value of 40 percent. Understanding the relationship between the attractiveness of refunding and the corporation's tax rate would be useful. Such an analysis could also show if the refunding decision is affected by ownership status.

As Aram's assistant, you have been asked to perform the refunding analysis and to report your conclusions and recommendations at the next executive committee meeting. With the model at hand you begin your work, noting that for ease of calculation the model assumes annual coupons.

Capital
Investment

BOCA GRANDE HOSPITAL

19

TRADITIONAL PROJECT ANALYSIS

BOCA GRANDE HOSPITAL is a 250-bed, investor-owned hospital located in Boca Grande, Florida, which is known as the "Tarpon Capital of the World" for its fine fishing. The hospital was founded in 1946 by Rob Winslow, a prominent Florida physician, on his return from service in World War II. Winslow relinquished control of the hospital in 1967 while it was still small and in a relatively quiet setting. However, in recent years, the Florida lower west coast has experienced a population explosion, which has fostered high economic growth as well as a continuing need for more healthcare services. Today, under a succession of excellent CEOs, Boca Grande Hospital is acknowledged to be one of the leading healthcare providers in the area.

Boca Grande's management is currently evaluating a proposed ambulatory (outpatient) surgery center. (For more information on ambulatory surgery see the Federated Ambulatory Surgery Association web site at www.fasa.org). Over 80 percent of all outpatient surgery is performed by specialists in gastroenterology, gynecology, ophthalmology, otolaryngology, orthopedics, plastic surgery, and urology. Ambulatory surgery requires an average of about one and one-half hours, minor procedures take about one hour or less, and major procedures take about two or more hours. About 60 percent of the procedures are performed under general anesthesia, 30 percent under local anesthesia, and 10 percent under regional or spinal anesthesia. In general, operating rooms are built in pairs so that a patient can be prepped in one room while the surgeon is completing a procedure in the other room.

The outpatient surgery market has experienced significant growth since the first ambulatory surgery center opened in 1970. By 1990, about 2.5 million procedures were being performed, but by 2002 the number had grown to over 6 million. This growth has been fueled primarily by three factors. First, rapid advancements in technology have enabled many procedures that were historically performed in inpatient surgical suites to be switched to outpatient settings. This shift was caused mainly by advances in laser, laparoscopic, endoscopic, and arthroscopic technologies. Second, Medicare has been aggressive in approving new minimally invasive surgery techniques, so the number of Medicare patients utilizing outpatient surgery services has grown substantially. Finally, patients prefer outpatient surgeries because they are more convenient, and third-party payers prefer them because they are less costly. All of these factors have led to a situation in which the number of inpatient surgeries has remained flat over the last few years while the number of outpatient procedures has continuously grown at over 10 percent annually. Rapid growth in the number of outpatient surgeries has been accompanied by a corresponding growth in the number of outpatient facilities nationwide. The number currently stands at about 2,700, so competition in many areas has become intense. Somewhat surprisingly, there is no outpatient surgery center in Boca Grande's immediate service area, although there have been rumors that local physicians are exploring the feasibility of a physician-owned facility.

Boca Grande currently owns a parcel of land adjacent to the hospital that is a perfect location for the surgery center. It bought the land five years ago for $150,000, and last year the hospital spent (and expensed for tax purposes) $25,000 to clear the land and put in sewer and utility lines. If sold in today's market, the land would bring in $200,000, net of all fees, commissions, and taxes. Land prices have been extremely volatile in the Boca Grande area, so the hospital's standard procedure is to assume a salvage value equal to the current value of the land. Of course, land is not depreciated for either book or tax purposes.

The building, which will house four operating suites, would cost $5 million and the equipment would cost an additional $5 million, for a total of $10 million. For ease, assume that both the building and the equipment fall into the MACRS five-year class for tax depreciation purposes. (In reality, the building would have to be depreciated over a much longer period than the equipment.) The project will probably have a long life, but Boca Grande typically assumes a five-year life in its

Position	Annual Salary	FTEs	Total Salary
Executive director	$55,000	1	$ 55,000
Director of nursing	45,000	1	45,000
Accounting clerk	35,000	1	35,000
Collections clerk	30,000	1	30,000
Scheduling clerk	25,000	1	25,000
Registered nurses	40,000	8	320,000
Nursing assistants	15,000	2	30,000
Transcriptionist	20,000	1	20,000
Total			$560,000
Plus 20 percent fringe benefit allowance			112,000
Total salaries and benefits			$672,000

TABLE 19.1
Projected Surgery Center Staffing Requirements

capital budgeting analyses and then approximates the value of the cash flows beyond Year 5 by including a terminal, or salvage, value in the analysis. To estimate the salvage value, Boca Grande typically uses the market value of the building and equipment after five years, which for this project is estimated to be $5 million before taxes, excluding the land value. (Note that taxes must be paid on the difference between an asset's salvage value and its tax book value at termination. For example, if an asset that cost $10,000 has been depreciated down to $5,000, and then sold for $7,000, the firm owes taxes on the $2,000 excess in salvage value over tax book value.)

The expected volume at the center is 20 procedures a day. The average charge per procedure is expected to be $1,500, but charity care, bad debts, managed care plan discounts, and other allowances lower the net revenue amount to $1,000. The center would be open five days a week, 50 weeks a year, for a total of 250 days a year. As detailed in Table 19.1, labor costs to run the surgery center are estimated at $672,000 per year including fringe benefits. Utilities, including hazardous waste disposal, would add another $50,000 in annual costs.

If the surgery center were built, the hospital's cash overhead costs would increase by $36,000 annually, primarily for housekeeping and buildings and grounds maintenance. In addition, the center would be allocated $25,000 of Boca Grande's current $2,800,000 in administrative overhead costs. On average, each procedure would require $200 in expendable medical supplies, including anesthetics. Although the hospital's inventories and receivables would rise slightly if the center is constructed, its accruals and payables would also increase. The overall change in net working capital is expected to be small and hence not material to the analysis. The hospital's marginal federal-plus-state tax rate is 40 percent.

One of the most difficult factors to deal with in project analysis is inflation. Both input costs and charges in the healthcare industry have been rising at about twice the rate of overall inflation. Furthermore, inflationary pressures have been highly variable. Because of the difficulties involved in forecasting inflation rates, Boca Grande begins each analysis by assuming that both revenues and costs, except for depreciation, will increase at a constant rate. Under current conditions, this rate is assumed to be 3 percent.

When the project was mentioned briefly at the last meeting of the hospital's board of directors, several questions were raised. In particular, one director wanted to make sure that a complete risk analysis, including sensitivity and scenario analyses, was performed prior to presenting the proposal to the board. Recently, the board was forced to close a day care center that appeared to be profitable when analyzed two years ago but turned out to be a big money loser. They do not want a repeat of that occurrence.

One of Boca Grande's directors stated that she thought the hospital was putting too much faith in the numbers. "After all," she pointed out, "that is what got us into trouble on the day care center. We need to start worrying more about how projects fit into our strategic vision and how they impact the services that we currently offer."

Another director, who also is the hospital's chief of medicine, expressed concern over the impact of the ambulatory surgery center on the current volume of inpatient surgeries. This concern prompted an analysis by the surgery department head, which indicated that an outpatient surgery center could siphon off up to $1,000,000 in cash revenues annually. When pressed, the department head indicated that such a reduction in volume could also lead to a $500,000 reduction in annual cash expenses.

To develop the data needed for the risk analysis, Jules Bergman, the hospital's director of capital budgeting, met with department heads of surgery, marketing, and facilities. After several sessions, they concluded that three input variables are highly uncertain: number of procedures per day, average revenue per procedure, and building/equipment salvage value. If another entity entered the local ambulatory surgery market, the number of procedures per day could be as low as 10. Conversely, if acceptance is strong and no competing centers are built, the number of procedures could be as high as 25 per day, compared to the most likely value of 20.

The average net revenue amount, with an expected value of $1,000, is a function of the types of procedures performed and the amount of managed care penetration. If surgery severity were high (i.e., if a higher number of complicated procedures were performed than anticipated) and managed care penetration remained low, then the average revenue could be as high as $1,200. Conversely, if the severity were lower than expected and managed care penetration increases, the average revenue could be as low as $800. Finally, if real estate and medical equipment values stay strong, the building/equipment salvage value could be as high as $6 million, but if the market weakens, the salvage value could be as low as $4 million, compared to an expected value of $5 million.

Jules also discussed the probabilities of the various scenarios with the medical and marketing staffs, but after considerable debate no consensus could be reached. To add to the confusion, one member of the medical staff, who had just returned from a University of Michigan executive program on financial management, questioned why the scenario analysis had to be confined to just three scenarios. "Why not five or seven?" he queried. Additionally, he said that the executive program had taught him a good way to assess the impact of inflation on project profitability, which is to create and analyze an inflation impact table, such as the one shown in Table 19.2.

To help with the risk incorporation phase of the analysis, Jules consulted with Mark Hauser, Boca Grande's CFO, about both the risk inherent in the hospital's average project and how the hospital typically adjusts for risk. Mark told Jules that based on historical scenario analysis data that use worst, most likely, and best case values, the hospital's average project has a coefficient of variation of NPV in the range of 0.3 to 0.6 and that the hospital typically adds or subtracts 4 percentage

TABLE 19.2
Inflation Impact
Table

		Level of Revenue Inflation				
		0%	3.0%	6.0%	9.0%	12.0%
Level of	0%	NPV	NPV	NPV	NPV	NPV
Cost	3.0	NPV	NPV	NPV	NPV	NPV
Inflation	6.0	NPV	NPV	NPV	NPV	NPV
	9.0	NPV	NPV	NPV	NPV	NPV
	12.0	NPV	NPV	NPV	NPV	NPV

points to its 10 percent corporate cost of capital to adjust for differential project risk. However, Mark was quick to admit that the risk adjustment factor is arbitrary and that it could just as easily be 2 percentage points or 6 percentage points.

Assume that Boca Grande has hired you as a financial consultant. Your task is to conduct a complete project analysis on the ambulatory surgery center and to present your findings and recommendations to the hospital's board of directors.

Optional: This case is well suited for the application of Monte Carlo simulation. If you are familiar with this risk assessment technique, and have access to the apppropriate add-in software, apply it to this case.

REHABUSA

STAGED ENTRY
ANALYSIS

20

REHABUSA is one of the nation's leading providers of outpatient rehabilitative medicine. It was founded in 1984 in Phoenix, Arizona, by a group of five individuals who recognized the need for cost-effective alternatives to traditional hospital-based healthcare. This vision has become the hallmark for the company, and it continues today to provide the highest-quality, most cost-effective care available. (For more information on rehabilitation medicine, see the American Academy of Physical Medicine & Rehabilitation web site at www.aapmr.org.)

In its quest to lower the costs of rehabilitative services, REHABUSA uses the latest in noninvasive treatment procedures, which reduces direct costs and results in quicker recoveries. In addition, the company encourages patients to begin aggressive rehabilitation as early as possible, which helps them return to normal functioning more quickly than under conventional treatment protocols. Studies have shown that this approach to rehabilitative medicine saves $0.11 to $0.35 of every $1 spent using traditional methods. In spite of REHABUSA's relatively short history, its strategy has worked wonders, and it quickly expanded from a local to a regional to a national company. Today, REHABUSA is a multibillion dollar, publicly traded company with nearly 1,900 locations in all 50 states, Puerto Rico, the United Kingdom, and Australia.

For several years, REHABUSA's board of directors has been considering expanding its service line to include sports medicine. The American College of Sports Medicine (ACSM) defines sports medicine as the physiological, biomechanical, psychological, and pathological phenomena associated with exercise and sports. (For more information on sports medicine, see the ACSM web site at www.acsm.org.) Because there is a considerable degree of commonality between rehabilitative and sports medicine services, expansion into this rapidly growing area of healthcare seemed natural.

REHABUSA's board is examining two proposals related to the expansion into sports medicine. Proposal A involves a single, large investment that would immediately give the company a national presence in sports medicine. In essence, all of the current rehabilitation facilities deemed suitable to offer sports medicine services would be renovated, equipped, and staffed, as required, to offer sports medicine services. The amount of capital investment at each of the company's earmarked locations would vary significantly, but the average cost is estimated at about $400,000 per facility. With roughly 1,000 locations identified as being suitable for the sports medicine business line, the estimated cost of Proposal A is in the vicinity of $400 million. Although the profitability analysis of Proposal A is only preliminary, its internal rate of return (IRR) is thought to be in the range of 20–25 percent.

Proposal B, on the other hand, involves a more deliberate, two-stage sequence. Stage 1 of Proposal B calls for a trial program in which only one of REHABUSA's nine regions would offer sports medicine services. If the results of Stage 1 meet the company's expectations, Stage 2, which calls for the expansion of sports medicine services into the remaining eight regions, would be implemented.

Proposal A requires a much larger capital investment than Stage 1 of Proposal B. However, Proposal B is more costly than Proposal A overall, even when time value is considered, because Proposal A's large upfront investment leads to greater efficiencies in contracting, construction, recruitment, and marketing. In spite of Proposal A's cost advantage, several board members are concerned about the wisdom of Proposal A because it requires that REHABUSA make a very large investment in a business line that is new to the company. Other board members, though, see no difference between rehabilitation and sports medicine services, and one board member even said, "healthcare is healthcare."

The primary task at hand now is to evaluate Proposal B, which includes the trial program and possible expansion into all service regions. To date, REHABUSA has spent $7 million to develop a sports medicine

MACRS Class	Recovery Year				
	1	*2*	*3*	*4*	*5*
7-year	14.3%	24.5%	17.5%	12.5%	8.9%

TABLE 20.1
MACRS
Depreciation
Rates

Note: For ease, these allowances were rounded to the nearest one-tenth of 1 percent. In actual applications, the allowances would not be rounded.

service concept that matches its approach to rehabilitative medicine. Of the $7 million, $2 million have been expensed for tax purposes, while the remaining $5 million have been capitalized and will be amortized over the five-year operating life of Stage 1. According to a specific IRS ruling requested by REHABUSA, if neither Proposal A nor B are implemented, the $5 million could be immediately expensed.

If it decides to go ahead with Stage 1, REHABUSA would immediately spend $2 million to perform local labor market studies to ensure that the locations identified for the sports medicine program could be staffed. The next step would be to buy the land needed at locations where totally new facilities are required. In total, land acquisition costs, which are assumed to occur at the end of Year 1, are expected to be $10 million. New construction and renovations at the chosen locations would take place during Years 2 and 3, and equipment would be installed during the last quarter of Year 3. Also, additional personnel, as needed, would be hired at the end of Year 3. The total amount needed for new buildings, renovations to existing buildings, and equipment (plus a relatively small amount for recruitment) is estimated to be $50 million. For planning purposes, half of this amount is assumed to be spent at the end of Year 2 and the other half at the end of Year 3.

Although any new buildings actually would fall into the MACRS 39-year class, for simplicity both the buildings and equipment needed are assumed to fall into the MACRS seven-year class. Appropriate depreciation allowances are given in Table 20.1. REHABUSA would begin to depreciate the buildings and equipment during Year 4—the year in which the trial sports medicine program would be initiated. The trial program would be evaluated during Year 6. If the results are satisfactory, the program would be expanded to the remaining eight regions. If the program does not meet expectations, it would be terminated at the end of Year 8. If terminated, the land would have an estimated market value of $10 million at the end of Year 8, while the buildings and equipment would have a market value of $30 million.

REHABUSA's marketing department has projected two demand scenarios for Stage 1. If demand for the sports medicine program is poor, total revenues are forecasted to be $40 million for Year 4—the first year of operations. However, if demand is good, revenues are expected to be $60 million. At this point, the best guess is that there is a 50 percent chance of poor demand and a 50 percent chance of good demand. If demand is good, revenues are expected to increase by 6 percent each year after Year 4. If demand is poor, revenue growth is expected to be only 3 percent.

In terms of operating costs, variable costs are expected to be 30 percent of revenues. Fixed costs (other than depreciation), which are expected to total $25 million in Year 4, are forecasted to increase after the initial year of operations at the anticipated overall rate of inflation— 2 percent.

If board approval for Stage 2 is given during Year 6, REHABUSA would spend an additional half billion dollars on land, buildings, and equipment to expand into the other eight regions. This expenditure would be evenly split between Years 6 and 7. As shown below, the net cash inflows forecasted for Stage 2 depend on the demand scenario:

| | Net Cash Flow | | |
End of Year	High Demand	Medium Demand	Low Demand
6	($250,000,000)	($250,000,000)	($250,000,000)
7	(250,000,000)	(250,000,000)	(250,000,000)
8	150,000,000	100,000,000	50,000,000
9	200,000,000	145,000,000	70,000,000
10	210,000,000	150,000,000	70,000,000
11	220,000,000	155,000,000	70,000,000
12	500,000,000	350,000,000	150,000,000

Note that the net cash flows are "bumped up" in Year 9 to reflect the cash flows from those facilities in the test region. Also, note that the project is expected to last beyond Year 12, and an allowance for the value of these future cash flows is embedded in the Year 12 cash flows.

The estimated probabilities of the Stage 2 demand scenarios are related to the response to the Stage 1 trial program. If acceptance is poor in Stage 1, there is a 10 percent probability that demand will be high during Stage 2, a 30 percent probability that demand will be medium, and a 60 percent probability that demand will be low. However, if acceptance during Stage 1 is good, there is a 60 percent probability that demand will be high during Stage 2, a 30 percent probability that demand will be medium, and a 10 percent probability that demand will be low. Of course, these expectations may change over time as new information becomes available. Furthermore, the actual demand scenario for Stage 2 is not expected to be known until midway through Year 8, after the program has been operated nationally for six months.

REHABUSA's current income tax rate is 40 percent, and this rate is projected to remain roughly constant into the future. The firm's corporate cost of capital is 10.0 percent, but REHABUSA adjusts this amount up or down by 3 percentage points to adjust for project risk. REHABUSA defines low-risk projects as those having a coefficient of variation (CV) of NPV less than 1.5; average-risk projects have CVs in the range of 1.5–2.5, and high-risk projects have CVs over 2.5.

One of the most important advantages of staged entry is that new information will become available throughout the investment period. REHABUSA's managers recognize this feature, and believe that they will have a better estimate of the Stage 2 probabilities and cash flows prior to making the Year 6 investment. Furthermore, even if Stage 2 is undertaken, there is some possibility that the project could be abandoned at the end of Year 8 *if the low demand scenario materializes*. If the project is abandoned at that point, the best estimate for the Year 8 cash flow is $400 million. The uncertainty of whether or not abandonment would occur lies more in the politics than in the economics of the decision. In the past, REHABUSA's managers were not so inclined to admit mistakes and cut losses, so some doubt lingers about whether the abandonment decision would be made even if it is the financially right thing to do at the time.

Assume that you have been hired as a consultant to analyze the situation regarding the sports medicine program and to make a recommendation to REHABUSA's board of directors regarding the best course of action. In addition to a detailed analysis of Proposal B, you have been asked to compare the relative merits of the two proposals (A and B).

CRESCENT CITY HEALTH SYSTEM

MAKE OR BUY ANALYSIS

21

CRESCENT CITY HEALTH SYSTEM is a large not-for-profit health-care holding company that operates both for-profit and not-for-profit subsidiaries in New Orleans and its surrounding area. The not-for-profit subsidiaries consist of four acute care hospitals (Metropolitan Memorial, River Bend, Metairie Memorial, and Kenner General) and one service company (SUPPORT). SUPPORT provides various services, such as food, laundry, and medical waste disposal, to the four hospitals. The single for-profit subsidiary, PROPERTIES, operates several for-profit businesses, but its primary business line is real-estate development, particularly medical office buildings.

Crescent City's CEO, Susan Richards, has been thinking about the company's printing situation for some time. Crescent City has a print shop, which currently operates under SUPPORT, that provides some of the printing required by the hospitals, but it does not have the capabilities to do all the work required. As shown in Table 21.1, Crescent City currently (2002) spends about $830,000 a year on commercial contract printing, some of which could be done in-house if Crescent City expanded its printing operation. Of the $830,000, about $132,000 represents graphics printing—annual reports, brochures, and other promotional material. Most of the graphics printing could be moved in-house, but about 10 percent of the work (for example, the four-color annual report) would have to continue to be done by outside vendors.

Conversely, only about 15 percent of the almost $700,000 in forms printing, or just over $100,000, could be moved in-house. This is

TABLE 21.1
Printing Currently Done by Outside Vendors

	Fiscal Year	
	2001	*2002*
Graphics Printing		
Mercury	$ 85,002.31	$ 7,727.86
Universal Color Graphics	16,982.44	12,588.00
Crescent Press	9,300.00	24,446.00
Southern Louisiana Printing	5,628.50	711.94
Pickett Press	3,526.14	2,337.10
Sir Speedy	1,962.58	8,939.50
French Quarter Printing	85.46	0.00
C & S Printing	1,161.00	0.00
Metairie Printing Service	0.00	75,292.83
Total graphics printing	$123,648.43	$132,043.23
90% to be brought in-house	$111,283.59	$118,838.91
Forms Printing		
Continuous	$223,826.43	$239,493.82
Stock tab	77,150.41	82,550.50
Labels	68,032.88	65,965.88
Carbon snap	97,563.27	106,283.44
Envelopes	61,096.52	62,435.89
Lab mount	5,095.35	5,126.33
Flat 1/2 side	42,266.69	40,986.45
Special	39,910.37	46,295.47
Oversize	1,458.19	0.00
Special service	1,190.00	2,743.98
Card stock	21,237.40	23,479.11
NCR flat	21,017.01	22,798.19
Total forms printing	$659,844.52	$698,159.06
15% to be brought in-house	$ 98,976.68	$104,723.86
Total vendor printing	$783.492.95	$830,202.29
Total to be brought in-house	$210,260.27	$223,562.77

because most forms printing requires very specialized equipment, and printing forms in-house is just not cost effective for businesses, except for very large ones. Crescent City's vendor print contracts (both graphics and forms) increased in dollar volume by about 5 percent (2 percent volume increase and 3 percent price increase) from 2001 to 2002, and this trend is expected to continue into the foreseeable future.

In fiscal year 2002, Crescent City's in-house print shop handled $42,837 in hospital billings. (To avoid any potential problems with SUPPORT's not-for-profit status, the print shop currently performs work exclusively for Crescent City's four not-for-profit hospitals.) The print shop bills for materials only, but because material costs represent, on average, 30 percent of commercial vendors' total billings, the print shop currently does about $42,837/0.30 = $142,790 in annual work on a commercial billing basis. The equipment in the print shop has a current market value of $230,000, and the print shop generates about $20,000 in annual depreciation expense when calculated according to Internal Revenue Service rules.

To move 90 percent of the vendor graphics printing and 15 percent of the vendor forms printing in-house, Crescent City would have to invest in additional printing equipment. The capital investment necessary for expansion can vary significantly depending on whether new or used equipment is purchased, the type of main press selected, and whether only essential or "nice-to-have" equipment is purchased. Table 21.2 summarizes the equipment capital investment requirements. Note that the old equipment would be retained if the print shop were expanded. Also, the new equipment would generate tax depreciation of about $25,000 per year and the required delivery van would cost $2,000 a year to operate (in 2002 dollars).

The print shop is currently located in a leased space adjacent to Metropolitan Memorial, the largest of the four hospitals. The cost of this site is $10 per square foot per year. The print shop occupies 2,000 square feet, and hence current building costs are $20,000 in annual lease payments plus an additional $200 monthly in utilities and insurance. Unfortunately, this site cannot be expanded, and hence new space is required if the print shop is to increase its capacity. Suitable space in a good location can be leased at the same rental rate ($10 per square foot per year), but the new print shop would require 3,500 square feet, increasing the annual lease cost by $35,000 – $20,000 = $15,000. (Assume lease payments occur at the beginning of each year.)

TABLE 21.2
Equipment Capital
Investment
Requirements

Item	Estimated Cost
Two-color press	$ 65,000
Two-color press (small) Model 9860	26,000
10-hole drill press	7,800
Futura F-20 folder system	13,000
Collator-stitcher, 12 bin	28,000
Bookmaker, Michael 1000E	5,300
Camera with processor	14,000
Paper plate, AB Dick 148	11,500
Three knife trimmer	12,000
Infrared dryer systems (2)	5,000
Delivery van	20,000
Miscellaneous items	5,000
Total capital investment	$212,600

In addition, the new space would require $30,000 in initial remodeling and an additional $100 per month in utilities and insurance (in 2002 dollars). Note that all leases are negotiated for a five-year period, so lease payments are not affected by inflation, which is expected to average about 3 percent per year.

The expanded print shop would require an increase in labor costs of $76,777; these costs are summarized in Table 21.3. Labor costs to run the current print shop amount to $50,000 annually, and all current print shop personnel would be retained if the expansion takes place.

After discussing the print shop situation with her CFO, Susan defined three possible print shop alternatives:

1. Close the print shop completely and use outside vendors for all printing.
2. Expand the print shop as envisioned. Essentially, this means expanding the print shop and performing all feasible work in-house. Under this proposal, the print shop would remain under SUPPORT, Crescent City's not-for-profit service subsidiary. Thus, there would be no tax consequences.

Number	Position	Annual Salary
1	Lead printer ($15.00 per hour)	$ 31,740.80
1	Delivery person ($8.00 per hour)	16,640.00
1	Clerical assistant ($7.50 per hour)	15,600.00
	Projected raw labor expense	$ 63,980.80
	Plus: 20 percent fringe benefits	12,796.16
	Total annual incremental labor costs	$ 76,776.96

TABLE 21.3
Incremental
Labor Costs
(2002 Dollars)

3. Expand the print shop as in Alternative 2. However, all printing activities would be transferred to PROPER-TIES, Crescent City's for-profit subsidiary. In this situation, capital expenses, such as depreciation and lease payments, would be tax deductible. The primary motivation behind this alternative is to permit the print shop to enter the for-profit commercial printing business.

Crescent City's corporate cost of capital, which is dominated by hospital operations, is estimated to be 8.0 percent. However, the company also computes divisional costs of capital for each subsidiary. SUP-PORT, the not-for-profit service subsidiary, has access to municipal debt that currently costs about 5.5 percent. Its target capital structure consists of 60 percent debt and 40 percent equity (fund) financing. Because SUPPORT has a captive business relationship with Crescent City's four hospitals, it has relatively low business risk. Consequently, it has a relatively low cost of equity, 13.0 percent.

PROPERTIES, the for-profit subsidiary, cannot issue municipal debt. The bulk of its debt consists of mortgage loans provided by banks and insurance companies. Mortgage debt, which is secured by pledged property, has a relatively low interest rate for taxable debt. Currently, this rate is 7.5 percent. The subsidiary's combined federal-plus-state tax rate is 40 percent. Because PROPERTIES competes with other property development companies, its inherent business risk is high, and hence it has a relatively high cost of equity—17.0 percent. However, its ability to use property as collateral for its debt financing gives it a relatively high debt capacity—about 75 percent. Crescent City's capital budgeting policy guidelines calls for all cash flow analyses to be restricted to a five-year horizon with zero end-of-project salvage values. The rationale is that estimating cash flows any further into the future is just too difficult.

It is now December 2002, and the print shop analysis is due in one week. Thus, for ease, assume that all capital investment cash flows, as well as lease payments for 2003, occur at the beginning of 2003 (the end of 2002). Then, the five years of operating flows occur from 2003 through 2007. Also, Crescent City's capital budgeting policy is to assume that all costs and prices that are not fixed by contract will increase at a 3.0 percent inflation rate. Thus, any 2002 dollar costs must be increased by 3 percent annually beginning in 2003. Furthermore, any 2002 volume amounts must be increased by 2 percent annually beginning in 2003.

In regard to the feasibility of expanding the printing business should it be placed into the PROPERTIES subsidiary, Susan discussed the profitability of commercial printing businesses with Mark Stanton, president of the Pelican State Printers Association, the state trade organization. Mark pointed out that the average printer in the United States has a before-tax profit margin of 5.3 percent, while the average in Louisiana is just over 4 percent. Return on assets in the industry is 7.5 percent nationwide and 5.1 percent locally.

If the print shop were moved into PROPERTIES, it would go after printing business external to the health system. Estimates are far from precise, but new business in 2003 could bring in as much as $25,000 in additional pre-tax earnings (in 2003 dollars). This amount could increase to $35,000 in 2004 (in 2004 dollars), given more time to advertise and build customer relationships. Although very uncertain, the pre-tax earnings that stem from external business are expected to increase by 5 percent per year after 2004, including both volume growth and price inflation.

Finally, Crescent City's purchasing manager has questioned the company's policy regarding external printing contracts: What is the company's current policy, and might a change in policy have a bearing on the decision at hand? The discount rate to use in the analysis has also been an issue under discussion. Susan believes that the discount rate should reflect the divisional placement of the print shop, but some staffers have disagreed with this view.

Assume that you are the administrative resident at Crescent City and you have been given the task of analyzing the print shop situation and developing a recommended course of action. In assigning the project, your preceptor indicated that a risk analysis was appropriate. When asked for more guidance, his response was this: "You know more about this sort of thing than I do; just do it!"

FRANKLIN TEACHING HOSPITAL

MERGER ANALYSIS

22

THE PATIENT BASE of Palmetto County, Florida, with a population of about 220,000, is currently served by three hospitals: (1) Franklin Teaching Hospital, a not-for-profit university-related teaching hospital with 525 beds; (2) Suncoast Regional Medical Center, a 200-bed for-profit hospital owned by Senate Healthcare, a national chain; and (3) Palmetto General, a 400-bed, not-for-profit, acute care hospital owned by Citrus Healthcare.

The service area has a total of 1,125 licensed beds for 220,000 people, or 5.1 beds per 1,000 population, which is higher than the national average of about 3.1 beds per 1,000 population and much greater than the roughly two beds per 1,000 population needed under moderately aggressive utilization management. Of course, as a tertiary care facility, Franklin Teaching Hospital receives patients from throughout the state, but the bulk of its patients still come from the local five-county area.

With an excess capacity of hospital beds, the status quo may not survive the changing healthcare environment. Indeed, Palmetto General has had some tough years recently, as evidenced by its number of discharges, which have fallen to 11,412 in 2002 from 12,055 in 2001 and 12,824 in 2000. Additionally, Senate Healthcare has been aggressive in building market share in other areas of Florida through acquisitions. With these factors in place, some consolidation in the local hospital market will likely take place, and the most likely result is the acquisition of Palmetto General by either Franklin Teaching Hospital or Senate Healthcare.

Palmetto General operated as a county hospital for over 50 years and hence developed a reputation for providing healthcare services to the poor. After many years of operating losses, the county concluded that it could no longer afford to operate the hospital. So, in 1983, the county sold the hospital for $1 to Citrus Healthcare, a not-for-profit managed care organization and provider, which by 2002 had become the state's largest integrated healthcare company.

Citrus Healthcare's major business line is managed care. Its numerous plans, including HMO, PPO, POS, Medicare, and Medicaid, serve over 400,000 members in 31 Florida counties, encompassing all of the major metropolitan areas. In addition to managed care plans, Citrus Healthcare owns nine different providers: two acute care hospitals including Palmetto General, two primary care hospitals, one rehabilitation hospital, one mental health facility, one hospice, one home health care provider, and one retirement facility.

Palmetto General is the flagship of Citrus Healthcare's provider network and as such the company has maintained the hospital well in spite of falling inpatient utilization. In fact, in recent years, Palmetto General has built a new, state-of-the-art HeartCare Center and a modern MaternityCare Center. Furthermore, Palmetto General operates a full-service emergency department and a medical emergency helicopter service.

In response to the current situation, Franklin Teaching Hospital has formed a special committee to consider the feasibility of making an offer to Citrus Healthcare to acquire Palmetto General. The committee's primary goals are as follows:

1. To place a dollar value on Palmetto General's equity (fund) capital, assuming that the hospital will be acquired and operated by Franklin Teaching Hospital.
2. To develop a financing plan for the acquisition.

In addition, the committee has been asked to consider two other issues related to the potential acquisition.

1. What is the best organizational structure for a combined enterprise? Currently, both Palmetto General and Franklin Teaching Hospital have separate boards of directors and management staffs. Of course, the

senior members of the board of Palmetto General currently are Citrus Healthcare officers.

2. Should the medical staffs of the two hospitals be integrated, and, if so, in what way? The medical staff of Palmetto General consists of local physicians, including many family practice physicians, while the medical staff at Franklin Teaching Hospital is almost entirely made up of specialists, and all are members of Franklin University's College of Medicine with responsibilities that go well beyond clinical practice. A new committee will be formed to address the above issues should Franklin Teaching Hospital's management agree to move forward with the acquisition offer, but some preliminary judgments are sought at this time.

As a starting point in the valuation analysis, the committee has obtained historical income statement and balance sheet data on both hospitals. Table 22.1 contains the data for Palmetto General, while Table 22.2 provides the data for Franklin Teaching Hospital. Note that both sets of statements focus on operating data, which are considered to be most relevant to the analysis. In addition, some relevant comparative data are presented in Table 22.3. Finally, relevant market data are contained in Table 22.4. (Note that the data in Tables 22.3 and 22.4 reflect late 2002 conditions.)

One of the toughest tasks that the committee faces is the development of Palmetto General's pro forma cash flow statements, which form the basis of a discounted cash flow valuation. Two basic questions must be answered before any numbers can be generated. First, what synergies, if any, can be realized from the merger and how long will it take for any synergies to be realized? For example, can duplications be eliminated? Both hospitals have "mercy flight" helicopters and both offer full emergency department services, even though the two hospitals are less than two miles apart. And, what is the impact of such operational changes on revenues and costs and hence on the net cash flows that Palmetto General's assets can produce? Second, once the consolidation takes place and all synergies have been realized, what is the long-term growth prospect for Palmetto General's cash flows? The answers to these questions, and others, form the basis for the pro forma cash flow estimates.

TABLE 22.1
Palmetto General
Hospital: Historical
Financial Statements
(millions of dollars)

	1998	1999	2000	2001	2002
Income Statements:					
Inpatient revenue	$ 81.624	$ 88.249	$ 99.010	$105.332	$110.384
Outpatient revenue	22.861	27.067	34.628	43.616	50.810
Gross patient revenue	$104.485	$115.316	$133.638	$148.948	$161.194
Allowances and discounts	33.699	38.626	44.622	51.198	62.006
Net patient revenue	$ 70.786	$ 76.690	$ 89.016	$ 97.750	$ 99.188
Other operating revenue	1.922	1.515	1.367	1.725	1.048
Total operating revenue	$ 72.708	$ 78.205	$ 90.383	$ 99.475	$100.236
Patient services expenses	$ 60.245	$ 73.858	$ 81.525	$ 90.645	$ 89.505
Interest expense	3.045	3.147	3.093	3.002	2.980
Depreciation	3.466	3.689	4.395	4.258	6.031
Total operating expense	$ 66.756	$ 80.694	$ 89.013	$ 97.905	$ 98.516
Net income	$ 5.952	($ 2.489)	$ 1.370	$ 1.570	$ 1.720
Balance Sheets:					
Cash and investments	$ 2.388	$ 1.538	$ 0.162	$ 0.185	$ 0.198
Accounts receivable	18.860	20.581	20.821	21.570	16.732
Other current assets	4.539	8.475	4.669	2.585	2.898
Total current assets	$ 25.787	$ 30.594	$ 25.652	$ 24.340	$ 19.828
Gross plant and equipment	$102.596	$116.694	$122.611	$133.499	$146.130
Accumulated depreciation	27.243	30.505	34.900	39.158	45.189
Net plant and equipment	$ 75.353	$ 86.189	$ 87.711	$ 94.341	$100.941
Total assets	$101.140	$116.783	$113.363	$118.681	$120.769
Current liabilities	$ 9.182	$ 13.584	$ 5.771	$ 10.689	$ 11.431
Long-term debt	33.572	47.302	50.325	49.155	48.781
Total liabilities	$ 42.754	$ 60.886	$ 56.096	$ 59.844	$ 60.212
Fund balance	58.386	55.897	57.267	58.837	60.557
Total claims	$101.140	$116.783	$113.363	$118.681	$120.769

	1998	1999	2000	2001	2002
Income Statements:					
Inpatient revenue	$238.510	$287.559	$328.047	$363.236	$398.997
Outpatient revenue	47.963	57.351	69.252	89.992	103.746
Gross patient revenue	$286.473	$344.910	$397.299	$453.228	$502.743
Allowances and discounts	82.053	107.256	128.645	170.058	185.301
Net patient revenue	$204.420	$237.654	$268.654	$283.170	$317.442
Other operating revenue	5.587	8.899	12.193	22.672	9.979
Total operating revenue	$210.007	$246.553	$280.847	$305.842	$327.421
Patient services expenses	$178.788	$207.596	$231.673	$254.704	$277.938
Interest expense	9.232	10.468	11.983	10.691	9.997
Depreciation	13.289	16.637	19.621	23.286	26.489
Total operating expense	$201.309	$234.701	$263.277	$288.681	$314.424
Net income	$ 8.698	$ 11.852	$ 17.570	$ 17.161	$ 12.997
Balance Sheets:					
Cash and investments	$ 17.918	$ 19.862	$ 24.660	$ 27.726	$ 25.220
Accounts receivable	66.212	72.989	99.867	100.297	97.494
Other current assets	12.315	16.771	20.741	20.542	22.757
Total current assets	$ 96.445	$109.622	$145.268	$148.565	$145.471
Gross plant and equipment	$348.288	$341.064	$335.313	$362.152	$400.546
Accumulated depreciation	75.139	76.575	90.056	109.468	123.567
Net plant and equipment	$273.149	$264.489	$245.257	$252.684	$276.979
Total assets	$369.594	$374.111	$390.525	$401.249	$422.450
Current liabilities	$ 42.437	$ 35.061	$ 39.511	$ 37.733	$ 39.817
Long-term debt	146.997	147.038	141.432	136.773	142.893
Total liabilities	$189.434	$182.099	$180.943	$174.506	$182.710
Fund balance	180.160	192.012	209.582	226.743	239.740
Total claims	$369.594	$374.111	$390.525	$401.249	$422.450

TABLE 22.2
Franklin Teaching
Hospital: Historical
Financial Statements
(millions of dollars)

TABLE 22.3
Selected
Comparative Data

	Palmetto	Franklin Teaching
Average age of plant	6.8 years	8.5 years
Licensed beds	400	525
Occupancy rate	52.7%	64.2%
Average length of stay	5.5 days	6.6 days
Number of discharges	11,412	19,748
Medicare percent	57.2%	29.7%
Medicaid percent	10.3%	13.0%
Medicare case mix index	1.51	2.13
Gross price per discharge	$11,688	$20,204
Net price per discharge	$5,850	$12,757
Cost per discharge	$5,703	$12,144

TABLE 22.4
Selected
Market and
Hospital Data

U.S. Treasury Yield Curve:

Maturity	Interest Rate
6 months	3.0%
1 year	3.5
5 years	3.9
10 years	4.5
20 years	5.0
30 years	5.1

Market Risk Premium:

Historical risk premium	7.0%
Average current risk premium as forecasted by three investment banking firms	6.0%

Market Betas, Capitalization, and Tax Rates
of Two Publicly Traded Hospital Companies:

Company	Beta	Debt/Asset Ratio	Tax Rate
Provident Healthcare	1.1	50%	40%
National Health Company	1.2	65%	43%

**TABLE 22.4
(continued)
Selected
Market and
Hospital Data**

Ratio of Stock Price to EBITDA per Share:

Provident Healthcare	6.1
National Health Company	7.9

Ratio of Total Equity Market Value to Number of Discharges:

Provident Healthcare	$7,000
National Health Company	$6,000

Proportion of Cash to Current Assets:

Large hospital average	5.0%

Note: The data in this table reflect assumptions to ease the case analysis, as opposed to actual data.

Assume that you are the chair of the special committee formed at Franklin Teaching Hospital to evaluate the potential acquisition. You must present your findings and recommendations to the hospital's board of directors. Note that Tables 22.1 through 22.4 contain far less data than normally available to parties involved in merger analyses, especially when the potential merger is friendly. In effect, the case discussion and accompanying data raise many more questions than they answer. You will be required to make a myriad of difficult assumptions to complete the analysis. Although you do not know much about Palmetto General's local market, you do know the current trends in the health services industry. Use this knowledge to help make judgments about the case. The quality of many, if not most, real-world financial analyses depends more on the validity of the underlying assumptions than on the theoretical "correctness" of the analytical techniques.

Note that there is no preferred solution to this case, so your case analysis will be judged as much on the assumptions used in the analysis as on the analysis itself. Finally, remember that numerous risk analysis techniques are available that can be used to give decision makers some feel for the risks involved.

BAY AREA HEALTH PARTNERS

23

JOINT VENTURE ANALYSIS

DEL MONTE HOSPITAL (the Hospital) is a 320-bed, acute care, not-for-profit hospital located in Monterey, California. It is well known as a leader in new technology and hence draws patients from as far away as San Jose to the north and Big Sur to the south. The Hospital contracts with the Seaside Radiology Group (the Group) to provide radiology services for its patients. Basically, the Hospital furnishes the radiology equipment and technicians and performs the tests, while the physicians in the Group "read" the results. Because the Group bills patients separately for the readings, there is no direct payment from the Hospital to the Group.

Assume it is now 1988. At the end of one of the monthly medical staff meetings, Dr. Warren Berg, head of the Group, presented a proposal to Mark Covaleski, the Hospital's CEO. The Group wants to form a partnership with the Hospital to purchase a biliary lithotripter, a device that uses shock waves to crush gallstones. Lithotripsy emerged in the early 1980s as a noninvasive way to shatter kidney stones: Patients are placed in a water bath, partially anesthetized, and then subjected to repeated focused blasts of shock waves transmitted through the water. By 1988, renal lithotripsy was well developed, and researchers were beginning to apply the same technology to gallstones, which are extremely common and affect about 20 million Americans. With about 300,000 cholecystectomies (surgical removal of the gallbladder) performed annually, biliary lithotripsy offers the prospect of a painless, noninvasive, and cost-savings alternative to surgery.

The biliary lithotripter, which costs about $1 million, has not yet received approval from the Food and Drug Administration (FDA), and hence it does not qualify for Medicare/Medicaid reimbursement. However, the FDA has granted approval to begin clinical trials. If these trials satisfy the FDA standards for efficacy and safety, the biliary lithotripter manufacturers would be permitted to freely market the technology. (For more information on the approval process, see the FDA web site at www.fda.gov.) The Group would be involved in lithotripter usage because radiologists must read the ultrasound images that are used to locate the stones and confirm that the treatment has been effective.

Mark had recently read an article on biliary lithotripsy, and he is supportive of the idea. Furthermore, Dr. Berg mentioned that he had talked to the president of Medical Equipment International (MEI), one of the biliary lithotripter manufacturers. During the conversation, MEI promised to give the Hospital exclusive purchase rights in its service area during the trial period, which is a process expected to take about two years.

The idea of being an exclusive provider of gallstone lithotripsy appeals to Mark, even if it only lasts for two years. First, by offering this procedure, the Hospital is reinforcing its position as the regional leader in new technology. Second, an early start would position the Hospital as the leading provider if the technology became available to competing hospitals. Mark does not believe that the Hospital's board of trustees would be willing to bear the entire risk of the purchase, but he thinks that they might be willing to go along with a joint venture. Thus, Mark asked Dr. Berg to look into the matter further and develop a specific joint venture proposal.

Mark had almost forgotten the matter when, two months later, Dr. Berg appeared with the following proposal: (Table 23.1 contains a summary of the proposed financing.)

1. A separate business entity, Bay Area Health Partners (the Partnership), would be formed.
2. The Partnership would have two general partners: the Group and the Hospital. The Group would put up $300,000 in capital and retain 60 percent management control, while the Hospital would furnish $200,000 in capital and obtain 40 percent control.

Capital Contribution	General Partners	Limited Partners	Debt Financing	TABLE 23.1
$ 300,000	Group			Partnership
200,000	Hospital			Financing
500,000		25 @ $20,000 each		Summary
1,000,000			Bay Area NB	
$ 2,000,000				

(The Group is incorporated, but it files federal income taxes as an S corporation. It would incorporate a subsidiary S corporation for the sole purpose of investing in the Partnership. S corporations pay no federal income taxes. Rather, as in a partnership, the income is constructively prorated among the owners and taxed as ordinary income.)

3. Twenty-five limited partnerships would be offered to local physicians for $20,000 each. The limited partners (the LPs) would have no liability beyond their $20,000 investments but, on the other hand, would have no control rights. (The Partnership is purposely restricted to 25 limited partners because a larger number would require a more complicated partnership registration procedure with the State of California.)

4. An additional $1 million would be obtained from the Bay Area National Bank in the form of a five-year term (amortized) loan carrying an interest rate of 8 percent. The bank would require the Partnership to pledge the equipment as collateral for the loan. In the event of default by the Partnership, the market value of the equipment would first be used to offset the principal balance, and then the Group would be liable for 60 percent and the Hospital for 40 percent of any remaining balance.

The $2 million initial capital infusion would be just sufficient to purchase and install the lithotripter and to pay the consulting, legal, and accounting costs associated with forming the Partnership. The Hospital would lease the Partnership the space for the lithotripter, furnish the technical support required to operate the equipment, and handle billing and collections. Of course, all services provided to the Partnership by the Hospital would be handled at "arm's length," and hence the Partnership would pay the Hospital prevailing market rates for the services provided.

The Partnership itself would not be taxed, but its distributions represent income, and hence would be taxed on the basis of each partner's tax status. The distributions to the Hospital would be nontaxable because the joint venture is consistent with the Hospital's not-for-profit status. The distributions to the Group and to the LPs would be taxed as ordinary income. However, about 50 percent of the distributions would represent a return of capital (depreciation cash flow), which is not taxed, and hence taxable investors would pay taxes at an effective rate of only about 20 percent.

The cash flows from the Partnership would be distributed according to the following plan:

1. The Partnership would distribute all earned net cash flow to the partners at the end of each year.
2. At the end of the first year, the general partners would receive 30 percent of the cash flow and the LPs would receive 70 percent. Following the distribution at the end of each year, the total accumulated dollar return provided to the LPs would be calculated. If this amount is less than the LPs' total contribution, they would continue to receive 70 percent of the cash flow in the following year.
3. In the years succeeding the year in which the LPs recover their initial contribution, 50 percent of the cash flow would be distributed to the general partners, while 50 percent would go to the LPs.
4. The cash flow allocated to the general partners would be distributed proportionally to the Group and to the Hospital on the basis of each partner's relative contribution: 60 percent would go to the Group and 40 percent to the Hospital.

Of course, the key to a sound financial analysis is good cash flow estimates. Mark and Dr. Berg devoted an entire day to the cash flow estimation process, and many other individuals provided inputs. If the joint venture gets off the ground, the lithotripter would be in operation by the end of the year (Year 0). The equipment would be available for 50 weeks each year, and the best estimate is that four procedures would be performed per week during the first year (Year 1).

Although only approved for trials, several third-party payers have expressed an interest in supporting the testing. If the technology is successful, biliary lithotripsy would significantly lower future costs for the treatment of gallstones. Based on discussions with selected payers, the Partnership is expected to receive $5,000 per procedure on average. Thus, the net revenue in Year 1 is forecasted to be $4(50)(\$5,000) = \$1,000,000$. Physician and public awareness would increase after the first year, and hence volume is projected to increase to five procedures per week during Year 2. Although FDA approval would mean additional utilization by Medicare/Medicaid patients in Year 3, at least one competing hospital would likely have its own lithotripter at this time. Thus, volume is expected to fall back to four procedures per week in Year 3, to three procedures per week in Year 4, and to two procedures per week in Year 5.

Projecting the trend for net revenue per procedure is difficult. On the one hand, building inflation increases into lithotripsy charges may be possible. But on the other hand, more and more patients are joining managed care plans, and these plans often negotiate discounts that are sometimes quite large. Furthermore, FDA approval would mean that Medicare/Medicaid patients would join the patient mix, but these payments could be set below the standard charge; indeed, such payments could be below costs. To be conservative, no inflation adjustments are applied to charge estimates.

Technology is moving quickly in this area, so assessing whether the lithotripter would have an economic life of more than five years is very difficult. For the same reason, estimating the machine's salvage value at the end of five years is also difficult. Because of the uncertainties involved, Mark and Dr. Berg decided to take a very conservative approach regarding the life of the Partnership. Thus, for planning purposes, they agreed to assume a five-year life for the Partnership and a zero salvage value for the equipment.

TABLE 23.2
Partnership
Pro Forma
Cash Flow
Statements

	Year 1	Year 2
Net revenues	$1,000,000	$1,250,000
Cash operating costs:		
Technician support	$ 10,000	$ 13,125
Clerical support	3,000	3,398
Rent	15,000	15,750
Insurance	10,000	10,500
Marketing expenses	5,000	5,250
Expendable supplies	4,000	5,250
Service contract	50,000	50,000
Property taxes	23,000	24,000
Administrative expense	30,000	31,500
Principal repayment	170,456	184,093
Interest expense	80,000	66,363
Miscellaneous expenses	20,000	20,000
Total expenses	$ 420,456	$ 429,769
Partnership net cash flow	$ 579,544	$ 820,231

Table 23.2 contains the pro forma cash flow statements for the Partnership for years 1 and 2. Note the following points:

1. Technician costs are estimated at $50 per procedure, so total technician support for Year 1 is (4)(50)$50 = $10,000.
2. Clerical costs are estimated at $15 per procedure, so total clerical expense for Year 1 is (4)(50)$15 = $3,000.
3. Technician and clerical salaries are expected to increase at an annual rate of 5 percent.
4. Rent, insurance, and marketing expenses are forecasted to be $15,000, $10,000, and $5,000, respectively, in Year 1. These costs are expected to increase at the projected inflation rate of 5 percent.
5. Expendable supplies are estimated to cost $20 per procedure, and hence the Year 1 total supplies cost is

$(4)(50)\$20 = \$4,000$. Further, the cost of expendables is expected to increase at the 5 percent inflation rate.

6. The service contract on the lithotripter is expected to cost $50,000 in Years 1 and 2, $75,000 in Years 3 and 4, and $100,000 in Year 5. These costs increase over time because cumulative usage increases the need for maintenance and parts replacement.

7. The Partnership will have to pay property taxes on the equipment, currently estimated to be $23,000 in Year 1, $24,000 in Year 2, $25,000 in Year 3, $26,000 in Year 4, and $27,000 in Year 5.

8. The Partnership's administrative expenses are esti-mated to be $30,000 per year. These expenses consist of accounting and legal fees, as well as reimbursement for management time spent on Partnership business. These costs are expected to increase at the 5 percent inflation rate.

9. Principal and interest expenses are based on annual amortization of an 8 percent, five-year loan of $1,000,000.

10. Miscellaneous expenses, which consist of the costs involved in the semiannual partners meeting, forms printing, expendable clerical supplies, and so on, are expected to be a constant $20,000 over the next five years. Mark and Dr. Berg are most concerned about the estimates for weekly volume, and hence they spent a great deal of time developing the following data:

| | Weekly Volume | | | | |
Case	Year 1	Year 2	Year 3	Year 4	Year 5
Worst	3	4	3	2	1
Most likely	4	5	4	3	2
Best	5	6	5	4	3

These estimates are based on the assumption that the biliary lithotriptor will meet the manufacturer's expectations regarding efficacy and safety. However, any problems in this regard could mean that the trials could be curtailed or even discontinued. Even if the trials were completed, failure to obtain final FDA approval would mean a whole new ball game. Assuming no problems during the trial and subsequent FDA approval, the best estimates for the probabilities of the above scenarios are 25 percent for the best and worst cases and 50 percent for the most likely case.

The current yield on 20-year T-bonds is 8 percent. Furthermore, a local brokerage firm estimated the market risk premium to be 7 percentage points. Thus, according to the Capital Asset Pricing Model, the current required rate of return on an average risk stock investment is 15 percent.

In addition to the efficacy concerns, all parties have expressed concern over two other issues. First, are there any indirect costs or benefits (i.e., costs or benefits that do not appear in the estimated cash flows) to any of the parties to the venture? Second, does the Partnership raise any legal or ethical issues?

Assume that you have been hired as a consultant to examine the feasibility of the proposed joint venture. You must assess the situation and prepare a report for the Hospital and the Group. Mark and Dr. Berg know that the joint venture will never be successful unless all parties are satisfied with the financial arrangements. Thus, they believe that an impartial analysis should be conducted to assess the risk/return potential for each party. Furthermore, if any of the parties do not appear to be treated fairly under the initial proposal, they seek recommendations concerning possible changes that might increase overall fairness and hence give the proposal a better chance of success.

In beginning your analysis, you recognize that there are several different cash flow/discount rate formats available for valuing businesses. In essence, the partnership analysis is merely business valuation but from the perspective of different classes of equity participants. To allow the analysis to include multiple equity perspectives, it is necessary to structure the cash flows using the free cash flow to equityholders method. Here, the focus is on the cash flows that are available for distribution to equityholders, so interest expense (and any other creditor flows) must be subtracted from the cash flow stream. (Note that this format differs from a typical capital budgeting analysis, in which debt flows are not considered.) Because the estimated net cash flows are equity flows, they must be discounted by a cost of equity. (Typical capital budgeting cash flows are operating cash flows and hence are discounted by the differential risk-adjusted corporate cost of capital.)

You also note that sensitivity analysis is not very useful in this situation because the unique cash flow distribution system confounds such an analysis. Also, internal rate of return (IRR), although useful for the base case, breaks down in a scenario analysis because some scenarios create non-normal cash flows. Thus, you plan to use standard scenario analysis techniques for your risk analysis with net present value (NPV) as the profitability measure. Furthermore, because the purpose of scenario analysis is to assess risk, rather than incorporate it, you plan to use a constant 10 percent discount rate for all partners in the scenario analysis.

AKRON FAMILY PRACTICE

PRACTICE VALUATION

24

AKRON FAMILY PRACTICE (the Practice) is a medical group practice in Akron, Ohio, which operates two walk-in clinics. (For more information on physician group practices, see the American Medical Group Association web site at www.amga.org or the Medical Group Management Association web site at www.mgma.org.) The Practice consists of five physicians, three of whom are board-certified in family practice and two are board-certified in internal medicine. Of the five physicians, three work full time, while the remaining two work half-time. The Practice is organized as a for-profit corporation, but for tax purposes the business is classified as an S corporation. (In an S corporation, the business pays no taxes. Rather, the business's taxable income is constructively distributed to the owners, who pay personal taxes on the income.)

The Practice was founded ten years ago by two physicians (the part timers) who wanted to have more free time than their solo practices allowed. Initially, the Practice had only one location, but a second was recently added. The downtown clinic, whose patients predominantly come directly from work sites, is open Monday through Friday from 8 a.m. to 2 p.m. The midtown clinic, whose patients mostly come from home, is open Monday through Saturday from 8 a.m. to 8 p.m. Table 24.1 provides basic utilization and payer data for the two clinics. With the current medical and clerical staffs, as well as clinic space, the Practice's patient volume can grow as much as 50 percent without the need for additional personnel or facilities.

TABLE 24.1
Utilization and
Payer Data

Average Number of Visits by Day:

	Downtown	Midtown
Monday	39	57
Tuesday	33	46
Wednesday	33	43
Thursday	34	44
Friday	33	28
Saturday	—	37
Total	172	255

Payer Breakdown:

	Downtown	Midtown
Employer	27.9%	12.5%
Cash/Credit card	25.7	35.7
Blue Shield	20.9	24.4
Commercial	14.5	18.8
Medicare	11.0	8.6
Total	100.0%	100.0%

The five physicians who make up Akron Family Practice own the business. However, the two founding physicians control the business: each has a 35 percent ownership stake. The remaining three physicians each owns 10 percent of the business. Because the controlling physicians are looking to fully retire in the near future, they would like to sell the business. The remaining owners are less enthusiastic about selling out, but as minority owners their alternatives are limited.

Preliminary work by a business broker has identified several potential buyers, including another for-profit physician group, a wealthy individual investor, and a local not-for-profit hospital. However, the Practice's owners do not want to enter into any negotiations without first obtaining an independent appraisal of the business.

The most recent income statement of the business, modified to focus on free cash flow to equityholders, is contained in Table 24.2. Free cash flow to equityholders, as typically defined in a business valuation

Revenues	$1,149,791
Operating expenses	1,069,076
Pre-tax income	$ 80,715
Taxes	16,143
After-tax income	$ 64,572
Plus depreciation	11,070
Less capital requirements	15,000
Net cash flow	$ 60,642

**TABLE 24.2
Akron Family Practice:
Historical Free Cash
Flow Statement**

Notes:
1. Operating expenses include depreciation.
2. The Practice uses no debt financing, so no interest expense is shown above.
3. At these levels of income, the Practice's effective tax rate (if taxed as a C corporation) is about 20 percent.
4. Operating expenses consist of a fixed component plus a variable component. The best estimates for this year are a fixed component of $800,000 and a variable component of $269,076.

Case	Year 1	Year 2	Year 3	Year 4	Year 5
Best	12.5%	11.0%	9.5%	8.0%	7.0%
Most likely	10.0	9.0	8.0	7.0	6.0
Worst	7.5	7.0	6.5	6.0	5.0

**TABLE 24.3
Revenue Growth
Rate Estimates**

context, is net income plus noncash expenses (depreciation) less capital investment requirements to replace worn-out and obsolete equipment and to support future growth. Note that the statement is based on an assumed effective average tax rate of 20 percent, which is the rate applicable if the Practice were to file as a C corporation. However, the tax rate that must be applied in any valuation analysis would be the marginal tax rate of the acquirer. Also, note that the Practice currently uses no debt financing, so none is shown on the cash flow statement in Table 24.2.

Of course, the value of the Practice is not a function of past cash flows but of future cash flows. Heidi Wilde, the administrator of Akron Family Practice, was given the task of estimating the business's future cash flows. The first thing she did was to estimate the expected revenue growth rates for the next five years; these estimates are contained in Table 24.3. Because uncertainty is significant in future volume estimates, and hence in revenue growth rates, three scenarios are presented. Although Heidi wanted to attach differential probabilities to the three scenarios, her best guess is that one scenario is as likely as another one. Regardless of the near-term revenue growth scenario, the Practice's long-term, sustainable growth rate is expected to be 5 percent.

In terms of costs, the Practice's cost structure listed in the notes to Table 24.2 is expected to hold in the immediate future, with fixed costs (including depreciation) increasing at a 5 percent annual rate. Furthermore, the Practice will have to invest roughly $15,000 each year (in Year 1 dollars) in new equipment under the most likely growth scenario, $20,000 under the higher growth scenario, and $10,000 under the lower growth scenario. Inflation is expected to increase these capital investment amounts by 5 percent per year.

Assume that you have been hired as an independent appraiser to place a value on the business. To use the discounted cash flow (DCF) methodology, it will be necessary to estimate the required rate of return on an equity investment in the Practice. Little market data are available for guidance, but the current yield on long-term Treasury bonds is 6.0 percent, while the historical risk premium on the market, which reflects the premium on an average-risk common stock investment, is about 7 percent. *Of course, there are significant risk and liquidity differences between direct ownership of a relatively small group practice and ownership of the stock of a large, publicly traded corporation. To complicate the valuation even more, control issues could arise in direct ownership.*

In addition to the DCF methodology, numerous other techniques for valuing small businesses are available. Two methods commonly applied to value medical practices are variants of the market multiple approach, in which some proxy for value—for example, earnings—is multiplied by a market-determined factor that best expresses the relationship of that proxy to equity value. For this appraisal, you have determined that recent purchases of family physician practices have been priced at 0.7-0.9 times projected revenue and (more roughly) at $250,000-$350,000 times the number of full-time physicians in the practice.

With this information at hand, your task is to place a value on the Practice. In addition, the majority owners of the Practice have asked you to be sure to comment on the following issues:

1. Does the valuation depend on who would make the acquisition? For example, would a not-for-profit hospital place a different value on the Practice than would another for-profit group practice? If so, what factors drive this differential?
2. If the valuation methods do not result in consistent values for any acquirer, explain (a) why the differences exist and (b) which method is the most believable.
3. Is there any difference in the per share values of the 35 percent ownership of the two founders as opposed to the 10 percent ownership of each of the other three physicians?
4. How does the fact that the Practice uses no debt financing affect the analysis, if at all? Does the lack of financial leverage make the Practice a more or less attractive acquisition candidate?
5. Would there be a productivity problem if the Practice is acquired? That is, will the remaining (and potentially newly hired) physicians be as productive when they are employees of the Practice as they were (and would be) as owners?

DESERT VIEW HEALTH SYSTEM

PHYSICIAN EXTENDER ANALYSIS

25

DESERT VIEW HEALTH SYSTEM (the System), located in Albuquerque, New Mexico, consists of six hospitals plus supporting services that, in total, provide the entire continuum of care. The main inpatient facility is a 650-bed tertiary care academic medical center, although the System also owns two rural 50-bed hospitals, two 125-bed community hospitals, and a 250-bed long-term-care facility. In addition to inpatient facilities, the System has many outpatient clinics and centers. The physicians that staff the System's inpatient and outpatient facilities are members of the academic health center's faculty practice (the Practice).

The Practice's vice president for Outpatient Services, Dr. Paul Phillips, is exploring the use of physician extenders in the clinics as a way of enhancing physician productivity and, ultimately, the Practice's profitability. As a start, three clinics are being targeted for evaluation: the outpatient surgery pre- and post-op clinic, the internal medicine (family practice) clinic, and the eldercare clinic.

In recent years, the role of physician extenders has evolved to the point where they are having a considerable impact on the delivery of care in many different settings. For example, physician extenders can perform more than 80 percent of primary care physicians' patient care duties, including taking medical histories; performing physical examinations; diagnosing and treating illnesses; ordering and interpreting laboratory tests; and, in some situations, prescribing medications.

The use of extenders allows physicians to treat more and higher-acuity patients, therefore expediting patient flow and increasing revenues. Also, because compensation for physician extenders is less than that for physicians, costs per patient visit can be lowered. In addition to the obvious productivity and economic benefits, studies indicate that patient satisfaction improves when physician extenders are used. In essence, they are willing (and able) to spend more time with each patient than physicians typically do. This extra attention often results in better quality of care (real or perceived) and higher patient satisfaction.

However, as the role of physician extenders expanded, it was inevitable that some conflicts would arise. The increasing recognition by third-party payers that extenders are as acceptable as physicians in providing many services means extenders are a potential source of direct competition for physicians, especially in hospital settings where nonphysician executives generally "call the shots." Still, physicians at many solo and group practices are using extenders to supplement and complement their work. Conversely, there remains a "hard core" of private practice physicians who view extenders as a threat to their gatekeeper position within the current health system.

The two primary types of physician extenders are advanced registered nurse practitioners (NPs) and physician assistants (PAs). Although NPs and PAs often perform similar tasks, significant differences do exist. NPs must be licensed in the state in which they practice. To acquire such licensure, an individual must first be licensed as a registered nurse (RN), then meet additional education and practicum requirements that generally lead to a master's degree, and finally pass a national certification examination in one of several specialized areas. (For more information on NPs, see the web site of the American Academy of Nurse Practitioners at www.aanp.org.)

PAs must graduate from an accredited physician assistant educational program and then obtain certification by the National Commission on Certification of Physician Assistants. The educational training for a PA is similar to that of a physician, but much shorter—historically only two years. Although PA programs traditionally offered either associate or bachelor's degrees, most programs today are moving to the master's level. (For more information on PAs, see the web site of the American Academy of Physician Assistants at www.aapa.org.)

The actual practice status of physician extenders has been, in large part, driven by state law. For example, some states allowed NPs to practice independently, while others mandated some physician involvement (collaborative or supervisory). With PAs, most states required that a physician be physically present (or electronically available) when a PA treated a patient. In addition, many states allowed NPs to prescribe all medications independent of physician supervision, while the ability of PAs to prescribe medications was much more limited. However, the Balanced Budget Act (BBA) of 1997 removed many of the limitations imposed by individual states. Now, both NPs and PAs are allowed to practice without the immediate availability of a supervising physician. Note, however, that NPs are allowed to practice under their own licenses, while PAs must practice under the license of a physician.

In addition to affecting practice status, the BBA also changed the amount of Medicare reimbursement for services provided by physician extenders. Prior to the BBA, Medicare reimbursed NPs and PAs at 75 percent of physician fees in some settings and 85 percent in others. Today, NPs and PAs are compensated by Medicare at 85 percent of physician fee schedules in all settings. Although Medicare reimbursement encourages the use of physician extenders, managed care companies do not always recognize the value of physician extenders, and hence reimbursement at the level specified in the BBA is not guaranteed.

Although it may appear on the surface that NPs and PAs are perfect substitutes for one another, the differences in educational background create differences in philosophies of care. Because NPs follow the nursing model of care, which focuses on health education and counseling as well as disease prevention, they have a special concern for the overall health and welfare of patients. Furthermore, NPs often specialize in particular areas of patient care such as anesthesiology, pediatrics, and women's health. PAs, on the other hand, generally follow the medical model of care, which focuses on diagnosis and treatment. Of course, these are generalizations that do not necessarily apply to specific individuals.

As the first step in the decision process regarding the use of physician extenders by the Practice, Dr. Phillips obtained the selected national average productivity, revenue, and cost data for physician extenders shown in Table 25.1. Across all outpatient settings where physicians and

Table 25.1
Selected National
Physician Extender
Productivity, Revenue,
and Cost Data

Productivity Data (Average per Physician for All Outpatient Settings)

Productivity Measure	Without Extenders	With One Extender
Office visits per hour	2.82	3.81
Patients visits per year	5,678	7,650

Revenue and Cost Data (Average for All Outpatient Settings)

Physician Extender	Revenue per Day	Cost per Day
NP	$570	$328
PA	719	351

Note: These data are for case purposes only.

extenders work side by side, physician extenders allow physicians to be 20–50 percent more productive, as measured by patient volume per physician. In addition, the billable work done by extenders creates third-party payer reimbursement that is roughly twice the amount of the extender's compensation.

In addition to the physician extender national data, Dr. Phillips developed the selected data regarding each clinic's physician staffing, productivity, revenues, and costs shown in Table 25.2. For example, the outpatient surgery pre- and post-op clinic has 2.5 physician FTEs who handle 7,560 patient visits annually, which generate $842,481 of revenue (collections). Annual compensation for the physician FTEs totals $485,000.

Assume that you have been hired as a consultant by the Practice to look into the use of physician extenders. Specifically, Dr. Phillips has asked you to (1) estimate the financial impact of using one or two physician extenders at each of the three clinics and (2) recommend the type of extender that is most appropriate for each setting. (These tasks are not trivial and might require assumptions and information to supplement the data presented in the case.)

As a start, you conclude that the national data presented in Table 25.1 must be modified to reflect the actual impact on physician productivity in the three settings. Although the national average increase in

Outpatient Surgery Pre- and Post-Op Clinic		TABLE 25.2 Selected Data for Three Outpatient Clinics
Physician FTEs	2.5	
Physician costs	$485,000	
Physician fees (collections)	$842,481	
Daily patient utilization	36	
Number of days per week	5	
Number of weeks per year	42	
Annual patient utilization	7,560	

Internal Medicine (Family Practice) Clinic	
Physician FTEs	2.0
Physician costs	$273,500
Physician fees (collections)	$523,290
Daily patient utilization	30
Number of days per week	4
Number of weeks per year	46
Annual patient utilization	5,520

Eldercare Clinic	
Physician FTEs	2.25
Physician costs	$335,000
Physician fees (collections)	$454,219
Daily patient utilization	23
Number of days per week	4
Number of weeks per year	48
Annual patient utilization	4,416

Note: Most physicians in the Practice receive compensation from the University in addition to the amounts listed in this table.

productivity is roughly 35 percent, there is no reason to believe that this amount is applicable to all three settings. Next, you plan to estimate how many additional visits might be generated at each clinic if one or perhaps two extenders are employed. Then, the impact on costs and revenues must be examined. Of course, it might be possible to use extenders to reduce the number of physician FTEs rather than to increase volume. This outcome should also be explored.

Dr. Phillips recognizes that you are working with a minimum amount of "hard" data. Thus, it is important that you make the assumptions used in your analysis very clear as well as supportable.

METROPOLITAN UNIVERSITY HOSPITAL

26

COMPETING
TECHNOLOGIES
WITH BACKFILL

METROPOLITAN UNIVERSITY HOSPITAL (the Hospital) is an 800-bed, acute care, not-for-profit teaching hospital affiliated with one of the largest public universities in the country. In addition to serving the primary and secondary clinical care needs of the neighboring population, the Hospital serves as a tertiary and quaternary referral center for the entire region. For the most part, referred patients seek specialty care that requires unique and often costly clinical expertise and treatment that is available only at select institutions. Thus, it is not surprising that specialty care programs provide the Hospital with about 75 percent of its net operating income.

The Hospital's Center for Digestive Disorders (the Center) is one of the most successful of the specialty care programs. It consistently ranks among the best programs in the country in the diagnosis and treatment of disorders of the gastrointestinal tract. The Center's excellent reputation is further evidenced by the extent of its research funding and its ability to attract patients outside the immediate service area.

The 20 gastroenterologists who staff the Center are physicians drawn from the faculty of the university's College of Medicine. Unlike private practitioners, who focus exclusively on the clinical care of patients, faculty physicians pursue a tripartite mission of clinical service, research, and teaching. It is the successful combination of these pursuits that has helped elevate the status of the Center.

The Center provides care ranging from gastrointestinal screening to the diagnosis and therapy of common and rare disorders to the referral of appropriate patients to faculty surgeons for the treatment of benign and malignant diseases. The Center encompasses three separate business units: an outpatient clinic, a hospital-based endoscopy suite, and a hospital-based motility (movement) laboratory. Each business unit operates as a separate cost center, and hence each unit maintains its own budget. However, from a patient perspective the care provided is seamless because the Hospital's patient management system expedites patient flow among the Center's three units as well to inpatient status when required.

Although the motility lab generates less than 5 percent of the Center's total net patient service revenue, it is a vital component. The lab currently performs 600 manometry tests per year. These tests measure the pressure (flow) along the gastrointestinal tract, which assists in the diagnosis of gastrointestinal disorders that cannot be diagnosed visually. The prevalence of disorders such as noncardiac chest pain, dysphasia, gastroesophageal reflux disease, and small bowel motility disorders make manometry testing beneficial to significant segments of the population.

Each test involves the insertion of catheters (probes) into a patient's gastrointestinal tract that relay data back to a computer work station for analysis. There are two technologies used in motility testing: water perfusion and solid-state. The Center currently has three water perfusion work stations dedicated to motility testing, each of which performs roughly 200 tests per year.

Both water perfusion and solid-state technologies provide relatively reliable data for diagnosis. Furthermore, net reimbursement averages $225 per test regardless of technology, and the current per-test operating costs are identical: $140 for labor, $30 for medical supplies, and $15 for administrative supplies.

However, there are distinct differences between the two technologies, the most important of which is patient venue. Water perfusion technology requires the patient to spend one day as an inpatient, while solid-state technology can be done on an outpatient basis. Thus, each test using solid-state rather than water perfusion technology frees up one bed-day for other purposes. In general, the space that is freed up by new projects or technology is called "backfill space," so any beds that would be made available for other purposes by replacing water perfusion with solid-state technology are called "backfill beds."

Although known for its state-of-the-art technology, the motility laboratory currently has some dated manometry equipment. The Center's medical director, Dr. Carl Forsyth, has made proposals in the past to update the equipment, but more pressing (and more profitable) capital needs within the Center have kept the proposals from being funded. However, one of the current work stations is becoming increasingly unreliable, which has inconvenienced patients and created backlogs. In addition, manometry demand has grown to the point where some patients are being referred to other providers to ensure timely testing. These factors have prompted the Center's administrative director, Edith Hargrove, to seek immediate approval for the acquisition of one new manometry system.

To begin the capital expenditure request process, Edith is currently reviewing quotes from various manufacturers of manometry equipment. Her research on quality and cost has narrowed the field of competing manufacturers to one: Digestive Diagnostics, Inc. A water perfusion work station, which Edith favors, would cost $25,000, while the nine catheters needed to properly equip the work station would cost $500 each. The new generation of water perfusion systems, but **not** solid-state systems, has lower per-test supply costs: $15 for medical supplies and $10 for administrative supplies.

On the other hand, Dr. Forsyth believes that the Center should purchase a solid-state technology work station. Regardless of the technology purchased, the existing unreliable water perfusion work station would be "junked," as it is no longer capable of providing satisfactory service.

Edith, who is a clinically trained nurse, questions the clinical necessity of solid-state technology, especially in light of its higher cost. Although the cost of the work station is the same ($25,000), the cost of the catheters is substantially higher: $6,000 for each solid-state catheter versus $500 for each water perfusion catheter. Nine catheters are required for both technologies, so the total cost for catheters would be $54,000 for solid-state technology versus only $4,500 for water perfusion technology. In addition, solid-state technology has higher operating (supply) costs than does the new water perfusion technology.

Dr. Forsyth agrees with the capital and operating cost estimates, but he argues that the higher cost of solid-state technology is justified for the following reasons:

1. Solid-state technology enables a technician to perform two tests in the time it takes to do one using water

perfusion; rather than performing 200 tests per work station per year using water perfusion, 400 tests could be performed with solid-state. This would shorten patient wait time for appointments, decrease the current four-month backlog for motility testing, and potentially increase overall volume for the Center from 600 to 800 tests.

2.   The current water perfusion technology requires close observation and correct body positioning during testing to ensure accurate data collection. As a result, each patient is kept in a hospital bed as an "observation" patient. Conversely, solid-state technology enables the tests to be performed on an outpatient basis. This point is of particular interest to the Hospital because under current operations every test using water perfusion is a bed-day that cannot be filled by a medical/surgical patient. Each bed-day by a "true" inpatient yields an average contribution margin of $520, whereas the bed-day contribution margin for a motility test patient is only $40.

3.   Solid-state technology is quickly becoming the standard of care; not offering it would damage the Center's reputation.

4.   Solid-state technology would enhance the teaching curriculum for residents and fellows and provide additional opportunities for research funding.

To his credit, Dr. Forsyth is a respected physician with a reputation for providing the very best of patient care and at the same time remaining aware of his responsibilities to do so in the most cost-effective way possible. However, he has been criticized in the past for lobbying Hospital administrators for medical equipment that, in retrospect, could be labeled as being nothing more than "toys" for himself and his colleagues.

Edith listened to Dr. Forsyth's case for solid-state technology. She believes he makes some good points, especially in regard to the clinical efficiencies of solid-state technology. Still, in an environment where resources are limited and maintaining a positive bottom line is increasingly important, Edith continues to believe that the cost of the solid-state probes is a financial burden the lab cannot afford, especially when reimbursement is the same regardless of the technology used.

The two technology proposals have been brought to the attention of the Hospital's COO, Belinda Brach, for resolution. Believing that a detailed financial analysis is the only rational basis for a decision, she has asked you, a recently hired financial analyst, to investigate the situation. Specifically, you have been asked to use capital budgeting techniques to evaluate the two technologies and make a recommendation on which one to choose.

In addition, Belinda provided some much needed guidance. First, assume that the life of both technologies is five years, and that it is unlikely that either the work stations or the catheters would have any salvage value after five years of use. Second, there is no good methodology available to estimate the additional number of tests (above 200) that might result from pent-up demand if solid-state technology is used. Volume might increase by 100 tests (to 300), but it could increase by as few as 50 or as many as 150. Third, it is very difficult to say how many of the bed-days that are freed if solid-state technology is used would actually be filled by medical/surgical patients. Again, without good data, she suggests that you assume that 100 additional medical/surgical bed-days would result, but this number could be as low as 80 or as high as 175. Fourth, standard practice calls for all capital budgeting analyses to assume a 3 percent inflation rate in both costs and reimbursements. Finally, the Hospital's corporate cost of capital is 10 percent and it adds or subtracts 3 percentage points to account for differential risk.

Just as you were about to start the analysis, the phone rang. It was the COO. She said that it was likely that she could put her hands on some additional funding to buy a second system, but the amount would only be enough to buy a water perfusion system. When you asked Edith what the lab would do with the second current system, if it too should be replaced, she said the Hospital could sell it for about $10,000 because it was only three-years old. Edith added, "You might as well crunch the numbers on the potential second system while you are at it."

Working
Capital

DOWN EAST PHARMACEUTICALS

RECEIVABLES MANAGEMENT

27

KATHLEEN GROGAN received her Ph.D. in pharmacology ten years ago from the University of Maine. While there, she became very interested in the business side of drug distribution and hence stayed on for an extra 18 months to earn an MBA. After graduation, she went to work for Criser Corporation, a major drug manufacturer, where she managed the development of a new nonprescription anti-allergy drug. Although the drug passed all FDA trials and was certified for general use, Criser simultaneously developed a similar drug that was cheaper to produce and equally effective in treating most, but not all, allergy symptoms. Thus, Criser decided not to proceed with production of the drug that Kathleen helped develop. However, Criser was willing to license production and distribution rights to another company. Kathleen thought that this might be a golden opportunity, so she quit her job with Criser to found her own company, Down East Pharmaceuticals. The sole purpose of the new company is to obtain the license for, produce, and distribute the new drug, which Kathleen dubbed "SneezeRelief."

Kathleen is currently working on the business plan that she will present at a venture capital conference to be held in Boston. The main purpose of the conference is to match entrepreneurs with venture capitalists who are interested in providing capital to fledgling firms. Kathleen has spent a lot of time thinking about how her proposed company's receivables should be managed; she is concerned about this issue because she knows of several small drug manufacturers that have gotten

TABLE 27.1
Down East
Pharmaceuticals:
Partial Sales
Forecasts
for Year 1

Month	Sales
January	$100,000
February	250,000
March	400,000
April	600,000
May	450,000
June	300,000

TABLE 27.2
Down East
Pharmaceuticals:
Partial Sales
Forecasts
for Year 2

Month	Sales
January	$200,000
February	350,000
March	500,000
April	700,000
May	550,000
June	350,000

into serious financial difficulty because of poor receivables management.

Initially, Down East Pharmaceuticals would sell exclusively to drug wholesalers in the Northeast that specialized in nonprescription drugs. If demand proved solid, the company would expand its sales area. Sales are expected to be highly seasonal: allergy drug sales are slow during the cooler winter months, but they pick up dramatically in the spring, when plant pollen levels reach a peak. Business falls off again in the summer, but it picks up in the fall when the ragweed season begins. Kathleen's sales forecasts for the first six months of operations are given in Table 27.1. Assuming the fledgling company receives financing and begins operations, Kathleen's sales forecasts for the first six months of the second year are contained in Table 27.2.

Kathleen does not plan to give discounts for early payment; discounts are not widely used in the industry. Approximately 30 percent (by dollar value) of the wholesalers (her customers) are expected to pay in the month of sale, 50 percent are expected to pay in the month following the sale, and the remaining 20 percent are expected to pay two months after the sale. Kathleen does not foresee any problems with bad debt losses; the wholesalers she plans to sell to have been in business a long time. Furthermore, she plans to carefully screen her customers, and she believes that these two factors will eliminate such losses. On average, Kathleen believes that 20 percent of receivables will contribute to profits, so 80 percent of receivables represent cash costs. Furthermore, the First National Bank of New England has indicated that its receivables financing would cost 10 percent annually.

In spite of her optimism regarding bad debt losses, Kathleen is concerned about the company's potential level of receivables, and she wants to have a monitoring system in place that will allow her to quickly spot any adverse trends if they develop. Kathleen's total sales forecast for the first full year of operations is 800,000 packages. Each package, which will contain 12 tablets, will be priced at $5.

Kathleen would like you, an outside consultant, to develop the following first year data for the venture capital conference:

1. The company's projected average collection period (ACP), also called days sales outstanding (DSO).
2. The company's projected average daily sales. (Use a 360-day year.)
3. The company's projected average receivables level.
4. The end-of-year balance sheet figures for accounts receivable and notes payable assuming that notes payable are used to finance the investment in receivables.
5. The projected annual dollar cost of carrying the receivables.
6. The receivables level at the end of March and the end of June. Note that the receivables level forecasts, and all forecasts required by the following questions, should be based on these assumptions: (a) the monthly sales forecasts given in Table 27.1 are realized and (b) the company's customers pay exactly as predicted.
7. The company's forecasted average daily sales for the first three months of operations and for the entire half year.

TABLE 27.3
Illustrative Uncollected
Balances Schedule
(thousands of dollars)

Quarter and Month	Sales	Remaining in Receivables	Receivables/ Sales Ratio
Quarter 1:			
January	$ 60	$ 12	20%
February	60	36	60
March	60	54	90
		$102	170%
Quarter 2:			
April	$ 60	$ 12	20%
May	90	54	60
June	120	108	90
		$174	170%
Quarter 3:			
July	$120	$ 24	20%
August	90	54	60
September	60	54	90
		$132	170%
Quarter 4:			
October	$ 60	$ 12	20%
November	60	36	60
December	60	54	90
		$102	170%

8. The implied ACP at the end of March and at the end of June.
9. Aging schedules as of the end of March and the end of June.

In addition, Kathleen remembered from her MBA program that uncollected balances schedules are superior to aging schedules in assessing receivables performance when sales are seasonal or cyclical. Table 27.3 contains an *illustrative* uncollected balances schedule. At the end of each quarter, the dollar amount of receivables remaining from each of the three month's sales is divided by that month's sales to obtain three receivables-to-sales ratios. Using Table 27.3 to illustrate, at the end of the first quarter, $12,000 of the $60,000 January sales, or 20 percent, are still outstanding; 60 percent of February sales are still out;

and 90 percent of March sales are uncollected. Exactly the same situation is revealed at the end of each of the next three quarters. Thus, the illustration shows that payment patterns have remained constant.

The uncollected balances schedule permits managers to remove the effects of seasonal and/or cyclical sales variation and to construct an accurate measure of receivables payment patterns. Thus, it provides financial managers with better aggregate information than such crude measures as the average collection period or aging schedule. Because of their value, Kathleen also asked you to construct uncollected balances schedules as of the end of March and the end of June. Furthermore, she has asked you to use the uncollected balances schedule to forecast receivables levels at the ends of March and June of the second year of operations.

Kathleen anticipates that the venture capitalists will ask some questions concerning both the interpretation of the receivables data and the sensitivity of the results to the basic assumptions. Thus, be prepared to thoroughly discuss the results of your analysis.

PLATTE RIVER HOSPITAL
INVENTORY MANAGEMENT

28

PLATTE RIVER HOSPITAL is a 230-bed, not-for-profit, acute care hospital located in Kearney, Nebraska. The hospital carries more than 10,000 different items in inventory that vary widely in price, order lead times, and stockout costs. (Stockout costs are all the costs, including higher costs of service due to scheduling delays or emergency replenishments as well as the costs associated with negative outcomes and potential lawsuits, that result from running out of stock of a particular item.)

Platte River uses the ABC method of inventory classification, along with a variety of inventory control methods, to manage its different inventory items. The ABC inventory classification system works in this way. Platte River maintains data on the average annual usage and unit cost of each inventory item, which typically is called a Stock Keeping Unit (SKU). Then, the dollar usage (Average annual usage x Unit cost) is calculated for each SKU. Next, these amounts are converted into percentages of total dollar usage, and the SKUs are arrayed from highest to lowest percentage. The SKUs are then divided into three groups (or classes), labeled A, B, and C using the general guidance contained in Table 28.1.

To better utilize the limited resources available for inventory management, the hospital's managers focus most of their attention on Class A items. The usage rates, stock positions, and delivery times for SKUs

TABLE 28.1
ABC Classification
Guidance

Classification	Inventory Value	Inventory Amount
A	60–70%	10–20%
B	20—30%	30–40%
C	10–20%	50–60%

in this class are reviewed on a biweekly basis, with control and ordering system data adjusted as necessary. Class B items are reviewed every quarter, while Class C items are reviewed semiannually.

Even though this process has served Platte River Hospital well, Julio Ruiz, the hospital's newly hired chief financial officer (CFO), thinks the hospital is carrying excess inventories. He notes that the hospital has never come close to having a stockout, even when it has been running near 100 percent occupancy. Julio believes that a thorough review should be undertaken of all Class A items, and that it might be possible to increase inventory turnover 25 percent, and hence lower inventory carrying costs, by trimming current stocks. To convince the hospital's CEO, Julio plans to perform a demonstration inventory analysis that focuses on the forms used by the Surgical Intensive Care Unit (SICU). Different forms are required for almost every aspect of SICU operations, including records of patient progress; requests for lab tests, blood, and medications; nurse and physician notes; and transfer/discharge instructions. Table 28.2 contains inventory usage and cost data on the SICU's 25 forms. To begin his demonstration analysis, Julio plans to conduct a new ABC analysis on the SICU's inventory.

As part of its commitment to supporting the local economy, Platte River Hospital currently uses a single, local source for all of the SICU's forms: Atwood Printing and Office Supplies (Supplier A). Supplier A requires a $25 set-up fee on each order, in addition to the cost per unit. The hospital is considering using a national supplier, Bateman Medical Office Products (Supplier B), which charges no set-up fee but does charge $50 to cover postage and handling. Supplier B takes three days to deliver the forms, versus only one day for Supplier A. Processing each order will cost the hospital another $25, regardless of which supplier is used. Thus, the total order cost is $50 for Supplier A and $75 for Supplier B.

SKU Number	Unit Size	Supplier A Unit Cost	Units Used Annually
50071	25	$31	3
50083	25	16	4
50084	50	18	14
50091	250	86	28
50100	25	22	4
50102	250	793	3
50122	250	196	2
50129	250	177	3
50131	100	122	5
50132	100	98	5
50138	100	26	9
50139	50	21	10
50170	100	$8	83
50172	100	44	4
50174	500	62	8
50193	25	2	66
50194	100	122	2
50206	250	11	279
50472	100	192	2
50475	125	551	4
50694	100	18	10
51060	100	102	6
53006	50	17	4
53104	**100**	**66**	**46**
57134	100	16	5

TABLE 28.2
Form Inventory Data for Platte River's SICU

Julio's ultimate goal is to use EOQ concepts to examine the SICU's form inventory situation and to select the supplier. His primary areas of concern are (1) the number of orders placed each year, (2) reorder points (in units), and (3) total inventory costs. As part of the demonstration analysis, Julio will focus on the form used to order blood products from the hospital's blood bank (SKU number 53104 in Table 28.2). The data associated with Suppliers A and B, as well as inventory carrying costs and other data, are summarized in Table 28.3.

**TABLE 28.3
Cost and Usage Data:
Blood Product Ordering
Form (SKU 53104)**

Expected annual usage	46 units
Cost per unit:	
Supplier A	$66
Supplier B	$60
Inventory carrying costs:	
Depreciation	0.0%
Storage and handling	17.1
Interest expense	6.6
Property taxes	0.4
Insurance	0.9
Total carrying costs	25.0%
Inventory ordering costs:	
Supplier A	$50
Supplier B	$75
Current safety stocks:	
Supplier A	2 units
Supplier B (estimate)	6 units
Delivery times:	
Supplier A	1 day
Supplier B	3 days

In addition to an analysis without safety stocks, Julio is also concerned about the impact of safety stocks on the decision. The hospital currently carries a safety stock of two units of SKU 53104 to protect itself against stockouts due to delivery delays and/or an increase in the usage rate. When asked how that amount was arrived at, the manager of the SICU stated that she didn't know, but that they had always done it that way. However, if the hospital decides to switch to Supplier B, she stated that it seems logical to increase the safety stock to six units to reflect Supplier B's three-times-as-long lead time. Of particular interest are the impact of safety stocks on inventory costs, the safety margins that such stocks would provide against higher-than-expected usage and shipping delays, and whether or not the current lead time for Supplier A and the estimate for Supplier B make any sense.

Also, Julio has heard the rumor that Supplier B is about to offer a 10 percent discount if the entire year's demand (46 units) is ordered at once. He wants to know what the impact of this discount would be on the decision as to which supplier to use. Also, it would be good to know how high a discount is needed to make Suppler B less costly than Supplier A.

Furthermore, Julio knows that it is unlikely that the forms would be ordered exactly as prescribed by the EOQ model, so he would like to know the impact of ordering variations on total inventory costs. Finally, Julio knows that Platte River's CEO has expressed some doubt as to the value of the EOQ model in making "real world" inventory decisions. "If I'm right in my concerns," he asked, "what other inventory control methods are available to us?"

Place yourself in Julio's shoes and see if you can conduct the demonstration analysis that he has in mind.

Other Topics

EASTSIDE MEMORIAL HOSPITAL (B)

29

FINANCIAL FORECASTING

EASTSIDE MEMORIAL HOSPITAL is a 210-bed, not-for-profit, acute care hospital with a long-standing reputation for quality service to a growing community. Eastside competes with three other hospitals in its metropolitan statistical area (MSA)—two not-for-profit and one for-profit. Eastside is the smallest of the four but has traditionally been ranked highest in patient satisfaction surveys. For a more complete description of the hospital, along with its 1998–2002 financial statements, see Case 1: Eastside Memorial Hospital (A).

As the newly hired assistant administrator, you have completed the financial and operating analyses (Case 1) assigned by Melissa Randolph, the hospital's administrator. In fact, your presentation to the board of trustees went so well that Melissa asked you to present the hospital's preliminary five-year financial plan at the next board meeting. To aid in the planning process, she provided the following information:

1. Given your knowledge of the historical situation for Eastside, current trends in the healthcare industry, and the competitive situation facing hospitals today, use your own best judgment to create the hospital's financial plan. Make any assumptions you believe to be necessary to create the plan, including assumptions about inpatient and outpatient volume growth, capacity constraints, reimbursement patterns, hospital staffing patterns, input cost inflation, and so on. Be

sure to completely document your assumptions in the report. The quality of your financial plan will be judged as much (or more) on the validity of your assumptions as on the mechanics of the forecasting process. (You have very limited specific information about Eastside, so use your general knowledge about trends in the hospital industry to make the forecasts.)

2. The emphasis should be on the forecast for the coming year (2003), but you should also create rough pro forma income statements, balance sheets, and statements of cash flows for the coming five years, including key financial ratios.

3. The five primary methods for forecasting income statement items and balance sheet accounts are (a) percentage of sales (in which a growth rate is applied), (b) simple linear regression, (c) curvilinear regression, (d) multiple regression, and (e) specific item forecasting. You may need to use several of these methods in your forecast. (Hint: Do not forget that spreadsheets have a regression capability.)

4. Use the financial analysis from Case 1 to help with the forecast if this case was assigned. Those areas where hospital performance has been poor should be improved, and your forecasts should reflect anticipated operational improvements where applicable.

5. Do not get so involved in the mechanics of the forecasting process that you forget to apply common sense to your forecasts. Think about what has happened in the past and what is likely to happen in the future in regard to utilization, prices, costs, and asset requirements. If the forecast does not make sense, modify it until it does. For example, a blind application of statistical forecasting techniques might lead to a forecast containing five years of net operating losses. Regardless of statistical "fit," such a forecast makes no sense because any hospital, if it expects to survive, will have to take actions to adjust either utilization or costs to ensure positive operating results. Thus, the "blindly" forecasted values do not represent what is

likely to happen in the future, even though they might be a perfect reflection of historical trends. Also, a forecast that is wildly optimistic probably needs to be modified because payers would react negatively if hospital profits rose dramatically.

In closing, Melissa gave you her view of a good financial plan: "First and foremost, the plan should consist of the pro forma financial statements along with a table that summarizes the amount of financing generated internally and any external financing requirements. Second, key financial ratios should be calculated, and the hospital's expected future financial condition should be assessed, with special emphasis on changes from the hospital's current condition. Third, make sure that your pro forma financial statements are consistent with one another. The last assistant administrator could not figure out that some balance sheet accounts—equity (fund) capital and accumulated depreciation—are tied to income statement items, so he did not last very long. Finally, be sure to make all your assumptions clear, and be prepared to answer questions from the board concerning the impact of changes in your assumptions on the financial plan."

GOLDEN GATE HEALTHCARE

CAPITATION AND RISK SHARING

30

GOLDEN GATE HEALTHCARE is a physician hospital organization (PHO) formed by Golden Gate Hospital and its affiliated physicians. Over the past five years, the PHO has had an annual contract to provide exclusive local healthcare services to enrollees in CaliforniaCare (the Plan), the local Blue Cross of California HMO. In last year's contract with the PHO, the Plan paid primary care physicians on a capitated basis, but it paid specialists and the hospital on a negotiated (discounted) fee-for-service basis. Now, the Plan wants to change the contract so that the PHO would assume full risk regarding patient utilization. In effect, the PHO would receive a fixed premium per member from the Plan, which would result in PHO revenues that are roughly equal to those received last year. However, given those aggregate revenues, the PHO could use any payment methodology that it deems best to compensate each of its three categories of providers, including capitation and fee-for-service.

The PHO's executive director, Dr. George O'Donnell, a cardiologist and recent graduate of the University of Wisconsin's Nonresident Program in Administrative Medicine, initially said "no way" to the proposal. However, the Plan has indicated that it will take its 50,000 members (covered lives) to the PHO's primary competitor if negotiations do not work out.

As detailed in Table 30.1, the PHO's medical panel currently consists of 249 physicians. To better assess the situation, Dr. O'Donnell

Specialty	Number in PHO	Estimated Need per 50,000 Enrollees
General medicine	42	20.9
Pediatrics	15	4.1
Total primary care	57	25.0
Anesthesiology	9	2.5
Cardiology	12	1.4
Emergency medicine	10	2.5
General surgery	13	2.7
Neurosurgery	3	0.3
Obstetrics/gynecology	27	5.4
Orthopedics	11	2.5
Psychiatry	19	1.9
Radiology	8	3.0
Thoracic surgery	0	0.4
Urology	5	1.3
Other specialties	75	10.1
Total specialists	192	34.0
Grand total	249	59.0

hired a consulting firm to estimate the number of physicians, by specialty, required to support the Plan's patient population of 50,000 under aggressive case management. The results of this study are also contained in Table 30.1. Note, however, that the PHO serves patients other than those in the Plan, so the total number of physicians required to treat all of the PHO's patients far exceeds the total amount of 59 shown in the right column of Table 30.1.

On average, the Plan indicated that its enrollees are hospitalized at a rate of 380 patient-days per year per 1,000 enrollees. It is clear that utilization, and hence cost, is driven by Golden Gate's physicians. However, an analysis of recent data shows that there is significant variation among physicians' practice patterns, both in their offices and in the hospital. For example, Table 30.2 contains summary data on physician-driven hospital costs associated with three common DRGs. Consider DRG 127 (heart failure). The PHO physician with the lowest hospital

DRG		Minimum	Average	Maximum
98:	Bronchitis/Asthma	$ 2,872	$ 4,018	$ 4,638
127:	Heart failure	9,271	10,319	11,394
373:	Vaginal delivery without complications	6,498	7,568	8,015

TABLE 30.2
Average Hospital Costs for Three Common DRGs by Physician

costs averaged $9,271 in costs per patient, the highest cost physician averaged $11,394, and the average cost for all physicians was $10,319.

To help in analyzing the Plan's proposal to capitate the PHO, Dr. O'Donnell requested data from the Plan concerning last year's actual payments to the PHO. When aggregated, payments to the PHO were approximately $100 PMPM, for a total annual payment of $100 x 50,000 members x 12 months = $60 million. Of this $60 million, 42 percent was paid to the hospital, 12 percent was paid to primary care physicians, 38 percent went to specialty physicians, and 8 percent was paid for miscellaneous "other services," such as durable medical equipment, nursing home care, and home health care. Under the proposal, the PHO would be responsible for providing the same range of services to the Plan's members as in the past. Some additional covered benefits, such as outpatient pharmacy and out-of-area services, would be handled separately by the Plan.

As part of normal operations, the PHO has a standing committee to identify and resolve differences among its disparate providers. When Dr. O'Donnell asked the committee for a short report on current problem areas, including the possibility of a capitated contract with the Plan, he was provided the following information.

Golden Gate Hospital

The managers at the hospital are very concerned about its profitability. Last year, when the Plan paid 75 percent of charges, the hospital barely broke even overall. Although no one knows for sure, the best guess is that the hospital lost about 1 percent on the Plan contract. The managers believe that the only way to control hospital costs is to create a subpanel of physicians for participation in the capitation contract. When asked how the subpanel should be chosen, their reply was to choose the physicians that would do the best job of containing hospital costs.

Primary Care Physicians

Most of the primary care physicians believe that they have been the losers under past contracts with the Plan. On average, primary care physicians received only about 60 percent of charges for treating the Plan's enrollees. Primary care physicians have been the only providers who bear the risk of capitated payments; they get the lowest compensation, and they believe that they have to work much harder than the specialists do. Furthermore, primary care physicians believe that the specialists supplement their own incomes by overusing in-office tests and procedures. Some primary care physicians are even talking about dropping out of the PHO, forming their own contracting group, and "taking the whole capitation payment from the Plan and contracting themselves for specialist and hospital services."

Specialist Care Physicians

The specialists believe that the primary care physicians refer too many patients to them. The specialists do not mind the referrals as long as their reimbursement is based on charges; they received between 80 and 90 percent of charges under last year's contract with the Plan. However, if they are capitated, the specialists want the primary care physicians to handle more of the problems themselves. Also, whenever the subject of subpanels is raised, many of the specialists become incensed. "After all," they say, "the whole idea behind the PHO is to protect the specialists." Both sets of physicians—primary care and specialists—agree that the hospital is hopelessly inefficient. "After all," said one specialist, "the hospital has been getting the lion's share of the contract monies from the Plan and they still do not seem to be able to make a profit."

To respond to the Plan's initiative, Dr. O'Donnell and the PHO's executive committee must grapple with the following issues:

1. What proportion of the expected $100 PMPM capitation payment from the Plan should be allocated to each component (i.e., hospital, primary care physicians, specialists, and other)?

2. What payment methodology should be used for each component? Should all providers be capitated, should any be capitated, or should some combination of methods be used?

3. What risk pools or other incentives should be put in place to help control utilization? Because the PHO as a whole is capitated, it is fully at risk for the utilization of services by Plan members.

4. Should all of the PHO's physicians participate in the contract, or should subpanels be formed? If subpanels are formed, how should they be constituted?

5. What other actions must the PHO undertake to increase the chances of successfully managing a full-risk contract?

In pondering these questions, Dr. O'Donnell and the executive committee were forced to face the fact that Golden Gate Hospital really needs this contract. If the Plan takes its business elsewhere, the hospital would lose 52 patients per day. A blow of this magnitude to the hospital's occupancy rate would force it into a major restructuring. Furthermore, all physicians would be hurt, to a greater or lesser extent, if the contract goes to a competing delivery PHO.

Assume that you have been hired to advise Dr. O'Donnell and the executive committee of Golden Gate Healthcare regarding its response to the Plan's proposal. At a minimum, your report should address all of the issues listed above as well as the concerns raised by the physicians and the hospital. Furthermore, the report must provide specific recommendations on how to implement this contract because the report will form the basis for an implementation plan if the contract is accepted. A general discussion about payment methodologies, risk pools, subpanels, and so on, is not sufficient.

Ethics
Mini-Cases

TRIGON BLUE CROSS/BLUE SHIELD

COPAYMENTS

1

WHEN MOST PEOPLE are told they owe a coinsurance payment on a medical bill, they simply grimace and write a check; but not Gerald Haeckel, a retiree from Richmond, Virginia. He wanted proof that he was not paying more than the 20 percent portion that his health insurance policy required. When his insurer, Trigon Blue Cross/Blue Shield, balked, the retiree besieged state and federal officials with demands for an investigation.

Gerald's problem with insurer-provider negotiated discounts began when he became confused by a bill sent by Trigon Blue Cross/Blue Shield. The bill was for Gerald's wife's lumpectomy, which is an outpatient surgery to remove a tiny breast tumor. Trigon's patient benefits statement indicated that the surgery had cost $950, that Trigon paid 80 percent, or $760, and that Gerald owed a 20 percent copayment of $190. But then Gerald received a statement of charges and allowances from the surgery center indicating that Trigon's share of the bill had been more than halved to $374 because of a "contractual adjustment." Gerald assumed that a mistake was made in the surgery center's statement because if it were correct his $190 copayment would exceed a third of the actual cost, instead of the 20 percent called for in his healthcare policy's patient responsibility section.

Gerald's scrutiny of the $950 surgery bill led to a surprising discovery. Although insurance companies frequently complain about being duped by fraudulent policyholders and providers, Trigon and dozens of other health insurers and managed care companies stand accused of a scheme to siphon off millions of dollars from their policyholders. How does the alleged scheme work? For surgery priced at $1,000, the typical plan might call for the insurer to pay 80 percent, or $800, which leaves the patient with a $200 copayment. But if the insurer has negotiated a 50 percent discount from the provider and does not pass any of the savings on to its policyholders, the patient's $200 copayment becomes 40 percent of the $500 actual bill, and the insurer's portion drops to only $300.

Trigon's responses to Gerald's queries stirred up more questions than answers. Norwood H. Davis, Trigon's CEO at the time, assured Gerald that he did indeed owe the $190 and added that the details of Trigon's provider contracts were "proprietary." In another letter, Norwood made a distinction between Trigon actually paying its $760 share of the bill and "discharging" it. Norwood added that although Trigon might try to persuade a provider to accept less than its $760 portion of the bill, a policyholder was free to do the same thing regarding the copayment. Gerald, who by that point was livid, replied, "suggesting that an individual policyholder negotiate with a provider for price concessions borders on the insulting!" and he threatened to take the matter up with state regulators.

At a time when consumers are expected to take more responsibility for their own healthcare, undisclosed discounts raise questions about the accuracy and honesty of information provided by insurers, providers, and employers. Indeed, providers often are contractually prohibited from disclosing discounts. The insurance industry argues that hiding discounts is not widespread and the Chicago-based Blue Cross/Blue Shield Association notes that no court has ruled for plaintiffs in a discounts-related case. It adds that none of its affiliates that settled such cases admitted to wrongdoing. Furthermore, Blue Cross/Blue Shield executives argue that the discounts benefit policyholders by reducing premiums. In some situations, they add, employers who share in the savings ask that discounts not be disclosed to their own employees. "We're not lining our pockets with anything because there is nothing to line our pockets with," said Joel Gimpel, a Blue Cross/Blue Shield Association attorney.

What do you think? Does this case present an ethical issue? If so, to which party (or parties)? If you could act as the ultimate authority on this situation, what would you do?

SILENT PPOs
DISCOUNTS FROM CHARGES

2

ACCORDING TO THE American Hospital Association (AHA) and American Medical Association (AMA), some third-party payers are bilking providers out of large amounts of legitimate collections by use of a billing scheme known as "silent PPOs." Here's how it works. A payer—say, an indemnity insurance company or a self-insured employer—receives a $10,000 bill based on charges from Oak Haven Hospital for treatment of a covered patient. The payer would prefer to pay less than the full amount, so it contacts a PPO broker, who searches a database to determine which PPOs have contracts with Oak Haven at discounted rates. The broker informs the payer that Oak Haven has a contract with, say, Friendly PPO that includes a 25 percent discount from charges.

The payer then remits $7,500 to Oak Haven, which implies that the patient is enrolled in the PPO even though the patient has regular fee-for-service insurance or belongs to some other plan that does not have a discounted contract with the provider. When Oak Haven receives the payment, it verifies that it has a contract with Friendly PPO that calls for a 25 percent discount. But unless the patient's records are searched to determine whether or not the patient is actually a member of Friendly PPO, Oak Haven will probably grant the discount to the employer/insurer. Thus, the payer receives a discount that the provider is not legally obligated to give.

The AHA and AMA refer to the practice as creating a "secondary market in contracted rates," which they believe to be "big business." According to the associations, some PPOs make their lists of preferred providers and rate discounts available to a wide range of providers and brokers for a fee. Indeed, several brokers who sell "silent PPO" discounts to payers operate nationally. Brokers may even supply payers with computer software containing a list of PPOs that contract with a particular provider along with the negotiated discounts, which allows payers to automatically search for provider discounts and then to re-price provider bills with the discounts taken. Brokers receive about 30 percent of the discounts saved and, often, will split their fees with the PPO that supplied the discounted rate information.

Given the difficulty in detecting silent PPOs, it is impossible to determine the amount of money lost to providers from payers using this scheme. However, it has been estimated that providers nationwide have lost between $750 million and $3 billion annually since the practice began in the early 1990s.

What do you think? Does this case present an ethical issue? If so, to which party (or parties)? If you could act as the ultimate authority on this situation, what would you do?

DEAL OF
A LIFETIME

CORPORATE OWNERSHIP
OF LIFE INSURANCE

3

So what is new in the life insurance game? The answer is corporate ownership of life insurance policies on employees. Wal-Mart has been spending about $1 billion a year in premium payments to buy about $20 billion of life insurance coverage for 325,000 of its employees. Other big-name firms, such as Winn-Dixie, AT&T, Disney, GTE, Nestle, and Procter & Gamble have been doing the same thing. Some (or even many) for-profit healthcare companies are probably doing the same thing, but no data are available to confirm this suspicion.

The product being bought by these companies is called corporate-owned life insurance (COLI), which is almost unknown outside of the insurance world. In fact, insurers typically call COLI "janitors' insurance," to distinguish it from the life insurance that companies often take out on key senior executives to help offset their loss to the company from premature death and from corporate-provided life insurance that is part of a business's managerial fringe benefit program. In fact, one corporate executive at Winn-Dixie was accused of calling COLI "dead peasants' insurance" in an interoffice memo. Needless to say, Winn-Dixie would not comment on the accusation.

Here is an overview of how COLI works:

1. A company takes out, say, a $100,000 life insurance policy on one of its lower-level employees. The employee may or may not have to agree to the policy,

depending on the state. If it is necessary to get employee approval, the company may offer to pay a small amount—say, $5,000—to the family if the individual dies while an employee of the firm or $1,000 if the individual has left the firm. This payment to the employee's family costs the employee nothing, so it is not hard to find willing participants when worker approval is required.

2. To pay for the policy, the company borrows the entire amount from the insurance company that issues the policy. Usually, the policies are single-premium policies, so only one up-front premium is paid. The company also borrows the money needed to make the interest payments on the policy loan, so no cash would flow from the employee's company to the insurance company while the policy is in force.

3. The company's bottom line is helped in two ways. First, increases in the paid-in cash value of the policy are reported as profits. Second, the company receives a tax-free death benefit when the employee dies, even if he or she has long ago left the company.

4. The company uses the tax-free death benefit to pay off the policy loan and to make the payment to the family, if one was promised, and then pockets the difference.

Most companies claim they use the money received from insurance benefits to pay for various employee and retiree benefit programs. However, this is very difficult to verify and there is no requirement to do so. Furthermore, each dollar from COLI that is used for employee and retiree benefits frees another dollar to be used for executive compensation and perquisites.

What do you think? Does this case present an ethical issue? If so, to which party (or parties)? If you could act as the ultimate authority on this situation, what would you do?

BAYVIEW SURGERY CENTER

PRICING/BILLING OF SURGICAL SERVICES

4

JOYCE GRIFFIN IS an accountant who is also an avid tennis player. One fall afternoon, after an inspiring win at the tennis club, she noticed a sharp pain in her knee. The diagnosis was a torn tendon, which could be easily corrected by arthroscopic surgery. After consultation with an orthopedic surgeon that she knew from the club, Joyce asked the physician to schedule the surgery for the following week at Bayview Surgery Center (the Center), a local outpatient surgery center.

Being an accountant and detail minded, Joyce called the Center as soon as the surgery was scheduled to provide the required insurance information and to ascertain the amount of the charge. The patient accounts clerk at the center quoted a charge of $1,500 for the surgery and told Joyce to bring a check for $300 the day of the surgery to cover the 20 percent copayment called for by her health insurance policy. Joyce paid the $300, and, fortunately, the surgery was a resounding success. In fact, Joyce was extremely pleased with the medical care provided both by the center and the surgeon.

The problems began the following week when Joyce received a copy of the bill that was submitted to her insurance company. Her eyes almost popped out when she read the total, $2,657, which should have required a copayment of $531. Equally strange was that the insurance claim form showed no sign of her $300 copayment; the "Amount Paid" space had a zero. Confused by the inconsistencies between what she had been told earlier and the claims form, she confronted the Center's business manager for an explanation. The best answer she could get was "This is just the way we do it. Everybody does it this way."

There are two ways of looking at this dual pricing of services. First, perhaps the Center is trying to give the patients—the "little guys"—a break; we might call this the "Robin Hood theory" of billing. Second, the Center might be trying to increase business by quoting a lower price to patients, and hence charging a lower copayment, but making up for the lower copayment by charging the insurance company more.

Neither of these possible explanations were very satisfying to Joyce, so she informed her insurance company and asked them what they planned to do about the Center's pricing inconsistencies. But much to her shock and disappointment, her insurance company did not seem to care. Even worse, the letter she received contained these sentences: "We don't print money; we handle money. Do not worry about us over-paying for services because you, the consumer, are paying for this."

What do you think? Does this case present an ethical issue? If so, to which party (or parties)? If you could act as the ultimate authority on this situation, what would you do?

JEFFERSON GENERAL HOSPITAL

MERGERS, ACQUISITIONS, AND AGENCY

5

MARK MILLER, CEO of Jefferson General Hospital, has some tough decisions to make in the future. Jefferson General is a stand-alone, not-for-profit hospital that has a long and proud tradition of serving the community in which it operates. It was founded in the midst of the great depression as Jefferson County Hospital and remained under public control for over 50 years. Then, in 1986, after years of losses, the county decided that it could no long afford to operate the hospital, and it subsequently converted the hospital from a public to a private entity. At that time, Mark was brought in as the CEO. After a shaky start, he was able to turn the hospital into a moneymaker. Still, he was very aware of the hospital's roots, and he made sure that the hospital continued its original mission of providing healthcare services to the needy, regardless of their ability to pay.

Jefferson General is the smallest of the three hospitals that serve Jefferson and surrounding counties; the other two are St. Vincent's Hospital and Northwest Regional Medical Center. St. Vincent's has religious roots, but it is now operated as a not-for-profit, nonsectarian hospital. Northwest Regional is owned and operated by a large for-profit chain. The combined capacity of the three hospitals is over 950 beds, but none of the three operates above 60 percent occupancy. Furthermore, managed care is starting to take hold locally, and hospital utilization trends indicate that the service area will need only 600 beds as utilization rates are squeezed down.

The most logical solution to the county's changing healthcare market conditions is a merger between two of the three hospitals, and Jefferson General is the hospital most likely to be acquired. Mark has been approached by the CEOs of both St. Vincent's and Northwest Regional concerning his interest in a merger. Although it was too early to speculate on the exact terms that might result if a merger takes place, past mergers in the region provide some insights into what might happen to Mark should a merger occur.

If the hospital were acquired by St. Vincent's, Mark would probably continue as CEO of the hospital, at about the same compensation as he currently receives. However, he would lose much of his autonomy and authority because he would now have to report to the system CEO, who most likely would be the current CEO of St. Vincent's. If the hospital were acquired by Northwest Regional, Mark would probably relocate to a CEO position at some other not-for-profit hospital because the for-profit chain usually brings in its own management team when it makes an acquisition. But Mark would not go away empty handed. He would probably receive a large "golden parachute" as a result of his job loss, which might include lucrative stock options, a lump sum payment, and a consulting contract. The aggregate amount of such payments could easily be worth many times his current annual salary.

Although the ultimate decision regarding the fate of Jefferson General rests in the hands of its board of trustees, the members of the board were chosen more on the basis of their community ties than on their business acumen. Thus, all those involved are aware that Mark's recommendations regarding the hospital's future will carry a great deal of weight in the final decision.

What do you think? Does this case present an ethical issue? If so, to which party (or parties)? If you could act as the ultimate authority on this situation, what would you do?

THE AMA VERSUS THE AAHP

GAG CLAUSES

6

IN AN ESCALATING struggle between physicians and managed care plans, the American Medical Association (AMA) has called on HMOs to remove all contract provisions that doctors believe prevent them from communicating openly with patients. In its declaration, the AMA's Council on Ethical and Judicial Affairs stated that the so-called "gag clauses" are an unethical interference in the physician-patient relationship.

Gag clauses, according to the AMA, prevent physicians from explicitly or implicitly giving patients information about treatment options that are not covered by the health plan or prevent physicians from referring patients to specialists (which presumably are more qualified) outside the plan's panel. Even if such clauses are not explicitly included in providers' contracts, some physicians claim that they have been deselected because of excessive patient advocacy. However, such accusations are impossible to prove because almost all plans have physician termination-without-cause provisions.

In response, the American Association of Health Plans (AAHP) blamed the AMA for adding to the public's confusion about gag clauses. Furthermore, they cited a 1997 GAO (General Accounting Office) study that examined 1,150 physician contracts with 529 HMOs and concluded that none used contract clauses that specifically restricted physicians from discussing all appropriate medical options with their patients. In fact, 67 percent of the contracts that had business confidentiality clauses contained specific "anti-gag" provisions that encouraged discussion of all appropriate medical options. The GAO survey concluded that these business clauses were not likely to have a significant impact on the practice of medicine.

The event that triggered much of the debate over gag clauses was U.S. Healthcare's termination of its contract with Dr. David Himmelstein after he criticized the plan's policies during a televised public debate. Although the HMO would not comment directly on Dr. Himmelstein's termination, U.S. Healthcare issued the following statement:

> Nothing in any U.S. Healthcare provider contract shall be construed to limit any doctor-patient communication that a physician deems necessary or appropriate for the care of the patient.

Also, Dr. Lee Newcomer, chief medical officer for United Health-Care Corporation, stated, "I don't know of any plan that has contract language that says a physician cannot discuss clinical alternatives."

But physicians have reported that HMOs threatened them with termination if they referred patients to specialists outside the plan. According to the AMA, many physicians are fearful that they would be terminated if they violated the gag provisions. "To those managed care plans still threatening the health of Americans with unethical gag policies, we say 'Why are you afraid of your patients receiving complete information on their treatment options?'" said Dr. Donald T. Lewers, a member of the AMA's board of trustees.

What do you think? Does this case present an ethical issue? If so, to which party (or parties)? If you could act as the ultimate authority on this situation, what would you do?

About the Author

LOUIS C. GAPENSKI, PH.D., is a professor in both health services administration and finance at the University of Florida. He is the author or coauthor of over 20 textbooks on corporate and healthcare finance. Dr. Gapenski's books are used world wide, with Canadian and international editions and translations in Russian, Bulgarian, Chinese, Indonesian, and Spanish. In addition, he has published numerous journal articles related to corporate and healthcare finance.

Dr. Gapenski received a B.S. degree from the Virginia Military Institute, a M.S. degree from the U.S. Naval Postgraduate School, and M.B.A. and Ph.D. degrees from the University of Florida.

Dr. Gapenski is an active member of the Association of University Programs in Health Administration, the American College of Healthcare Executives, and the Healthcare Financial Management Association. He has acted as academic advisor, chaired sessions, and presented papers at numerous national meetings. Additionally, Dr. Gapenski has received numerous teaching awards and has acted as a reviewer for many academic and professional journals.